WHAT PEOPLE ARE SAYING
ABOUT THE LAST LIE

Ms. Jefferis adeptly uses her own life experiences to explore the forces and complications which women experience as they grow and develop in contemporary society. Her path takes her to a deeper and more profound spiritual experience, which ultimately lends itself to an awareness of God's love. Many women will resonate with her experience, her understandings and her insights."

—GLORIA J. STERLING, PH.D.

For most of us, we work hard at staying busy, staying productive, staying disconnected from ourselves. At the same time, we long for the deeper, more meaningful connections in our relationship with self and others. Through Jennifer's life story, we see that with the courage to do the hard work, through reflecting and learning our lessons, we can deepen the connection to our core self, to our spiritual self. Her history may be a familiar one but her journey to self is a "must read" for any woman who has experienced disillusionment and dreams of a better life, a life of meaning. Having been friends since childhood, I've witnessed the courage, the determination and the grace

that continues to transform Jennifer and those around her,
I'm humbled."

—SANDRA WRIGHT, BUSINESS & LIFE COACH

    *A thought-provoking book with significant
messages of wisdom and hope for every reader. The story
is autobiographical and riveting and describes a personal
journey from despair to hope and clarity. Ms. Jefferis is a
gifted poet and the soft yet profound poems, even in their
few lines at the top of each chapter, serve as a daunting
foreshadowing of what is ahead for the reader. You will
not be able to put this book aside...you will be bonded to
the story early and tightly."*

—BONNIE WEDEKING MURRAY, PSYCHOTHERAPIST

    *Out of the painfully real yet revealing events of
her own life, Jennifer Jefferis traces her search for health,
meaning and joy. With compassion and honesty, Jefferis
explores both the wounds of the past and the deep hopes
that led her forward. She models for the rest of us how
to seek and find the personal well-being and satisfying
relationships that God wants for all of us."*

—REV. RICHARD JAECH, BISHOP, SOUTHWESTERN
WASHINGTON SYNOD, EVANGELICAL
LUTHERAN CHURCH IN AMERICA

THE LAST LIE

LIGHT RIBBON PRESS

The Last Lie: Finding Love After Betrayal
© 2014 by Jennifer Jefferis

ISBN: 978-0-9903520-0-6

Printed in the United States of America

WWW.EMBRACINGABETTERLIFE.COM

THE
LAST
LIE

FINDING LOVE AFTER BETRAYAL

JENNIFER JEFFERIS

CONTENTS

PROLOGUE   IX

ACKNOWLEDGEMENTS   XIII

INTRODUCTION   XIX

CHAPTER ONE: *The Unfolding*   1

CHAPTER TWO: *A New Heart*   11

CHAPTER THREE: *The Garden of Empathy*   23

CHAPTER FOUR: *Roles and Scripts*   31

CHAPTER FIVE: *Lost*   43

CHAPTER SIX: *Sweet Sixteen*   53

CHAPTER SEVEN: *Where Are You?*   65

CHAPTER EIGHT: *The Desire to Be Loved*   77

CHAPTER NINE: *The Best and the Worst*   85

CHAPTER TEN: *A Sudden Change in Plans*   95

CHAPTER ELEVEN: *The Last Lie*   103

CHAPTER TWELVE: *Lucky Me*   109

EPILOGUE: *Old Dragons*   117

PROLOGUE

It is spring in the Northwest and as I write it is raining. It has been raining steadily for weeks. Nothing too unusual about this when you live in one of the greenest regions of the United States. It amazes me when someone states, "I love the rain!" I want to gag them, for fear it will only bring more. Yet I find myself marveling at their ability to love being right where they are. Right where they are, right now. So even though their words set me back on my heels a bit, I admire their position.

Loving where you are right now is like having the capacity to hold onto life with a full body hug! My faith in God has taught me how to say yes to life and embrace all the things I am grateful for each day. I look back at the journey of my life and breathe in the gift of life today. I have learned each morning to simply rise and be grateful. In life, having that means everything.

Courage is a strange thing, and it takes a whole lot less than you think to change your life. Just a little courage gives you the ability to begin. For me, and for many of the women I meet and counsel, finding a little courage is all it takes to get started on having a better life.

Ribbons in the Light

Ribbons in the Light
Ribbons yellow, red, orange
Ribbons of health, strength, life
Ribbons that flow in the air
Flowing with the light
Taking me on their stream
Waking up a soul that has been dying
Back to life anew
Treat her with kindness
Keep her strong and vigilant
Allow her to finally blossom
Watch for her
She is growing
She has a stalk that is strong
She will withstand challenges and discouragement
Help her know when it is time
To rest and care for herself

ACKNOWLEDGEMENTS

Without the many clients who held the courage to come through my door and ask for help, I would have never known the real heroes in my life. Thank you for your willingness to share your stories with me and explore ways to make your life better. Your hard work and determination still inspire me.

When I began to write this book I searched so many sources for how to start. I read books of famous authors, went to writer's conferences, classes and poetry readings. I remember how my first poem was written on a day when I was so discouraged. It was on that same day my dear friend Bonnie Murray sent me a card of support. Her card validated the words in the poem serving as a foundation for the many years I would spend writing this book. Her friendship held fast through the struggles we would both endure as I recovered from a difficult divorce and she weathered the sorrow of her husband's death to leukemia. Between the two of us we made it through and supported one another into the new lives we now enjoy.

Sandra Wright coached me during the times of change when I was recreating my professional life. She helped me to develop the skills I needed to leave a job and go into full time private practice as a psychotherapist. Her words pressed me to stretch myself and taught me the business end of being a therapist. My heart overflows with gratitude for her professional guidance and direction.

Sharon Matthews was always willing to lend a shoulder to lean on and an ear to listen. For the many nights she would have me come to sleep over and offered me a safe place to heal in her hot tub. What a respite in a time of great challenge. You are the best Sharon!

Dan and Sharon Stevens generously offered encouragement, hospitality and friendship by asking me to dinner at their home and being available to encourage and support me at all times. How can I ever thank you enough?

Jack and Carol Mumford opened their vacation home in a small rural town near Mount Hood to me whenever I needed to have some time away. I thank you from the bottom of my heart for your generosity and loving kindness.

Jim Dwyer and Christine Green, my patient writing cohorts who published books way ahead of me. Being with the two of you through all those hours of review was a gift. I will covet our time forever.

Laura Meehan, my editor whose patience and gentle, guiding manner sustained me through the process of learning how to be a writer. I am so glad I found you. You showed such kindness and professionalism.

I count myself incredibly lucky for finding my book designer, Brion Sausser. His many years of experience give him the ability to be a patient guide through the process of publishing. Thank you so much for your wisdom Brion.

And out of all the people on earth I have been blessed beyond my expectations through the loving support of my husband Lyle Larson. Getting to be with you and love you has been the joy of my lifetime. Together we dream dreams that come true. Our love teaches me every day what love is meant to be.

And to my three sons Chad, Jason and Nick for inspiring me and helping me grow up right along with them. I am grateful they showed me the way through their patience and love.

Worth the Risk

Risks come now and then
To awaken us
Remind us who we are
And who we want to be

INTRODUCTION

Several years ago, I saw myself in a woman who came to see me. I watched as she sat on the edge of her chair, pensive yet intense, curious yet restrained, discouraged yet eager to find a way forward. She was resolute about putting a stop to the emotional turmoil in her life.

Much like her, I found something inside of me unraveling early in my forties, and I was determined to figure out what I needed to do about it. For so many years I had held onto beliefs that were no longer working in my adult life. I struggled between the desire to remain in the life I was living and the desire to live the life I yearned to live. Like so many women I see in my practice, I wanted to figure out a better way, because something inside of me said it was possible.

I knew I needed to recognize and claim my own voice as an adult, learn how to deal with my fears, and claim my own internal navigation system in order to stop feeling lost and afraid. I began to realize how not using my own voice as a guide for all those years was affecting my life. Now I wanted to pay attention to how my own wisdom desperately yearned to grow me up. I was sick of being a fear-filled child in an adult body, where I kept myself in lockdown, unable to see or consider options and choices.

At that point in my life, I began to see how I was repeating my history from my family of origin. I was unhappy, discouraged, disappointed, and felt trapped. I was beginning to recognize that there had to be something better for me; I could not tolerate the pain any longer. Through all the years of diligently trying to make things work in my marriage, raise my children, and grow up myself, my past was catching up with me—my desire to change forced me to face what I had fled as a young girl. The emotional pain of witnessing the ongoing physical abuse my father inflicted on my older sister Becky was terrifying to me as a young girl, and watching my mother stand by and not protect her was even more hurtful.

As an adult, I came to understand that I had grown up in a home where my two older sisters' mental health issues left little time or attention for me and my younger sister Lynn. I learned that it was bipolar disorder that had decimated our lives with chaos and unpredictability. Living in fear of what might happen next flooded me with an uncertainty that stayed with me long into my adulthood.

As an adult, I knew I wanted more than what I had lived through as a child. I wanted to have a life where I felt loved, safe, and cared for and I wanted to figure out how to do that. As I began to examine how I had got to this point, I knew it would take exploring my past to understand and learn how to create my future.

My relationship with my husband, a high school sweetheart whom I had met when I was sixteen, was for the most part intolerable. At one time, our relationship served to numb the experience of what I knew at home. I thought having a life with someone like him would give me a way to find joy. Being with him seemed to hold everything my heart desired. He was good looking, popular, and the center of attention at parties and at school, and when I met him, I believed all my desperate wishes were coming true. I wanted to find a peace within myself, but I did not know how. In my childlike thinking, I lost myself in him and escaped what I hated at home.

The constant unpredictability of my family included an abusive father, a submissive mother, and two sisters with bipolar disorder. My parents were too busy taking care of my older sisters to recognize that I existed, so it was easy to get swept up by my boyfriend or anyone who would show me attention. As time passed, I became numb to myself and lost direction of where I was going in my own life.

Blinded to my sense of self and driven to be free from my family, where I felt no sense of belonging, all I could hope for was that my life with him would be better. At seventeen, I found myself pregnant and married, and then my new responsibilities began to collide with the reality of my decisions. I was a young teen, living in a different town and separated from all I had known in the past. With no friends, with no comprehension of how to navigate my future, and alone most of the time, I was utterly lost.

As the years passed and I began to mature and change, I started to take a hard look at the strategies I had once used to survive, and decided to make different choices. The new decisions I would need to make would be tough ones, especially when the man sleeping beside me did not share the same values and visions I held for the future. As an adult, with three sons whom I loved dearly, I knew I still had a lot to learn. What I longed to give them and what I gave them fell far short of what I wanted them to have. I was skeptical about what I could do to help myself. Unsure and hidden deep under the scars of past trauma, a small voice was becoming louder. It was calling me to listen and giving me hope.

It was a huge risk when I stepped out in search of help. I was taught to keep my problems hidden, and in my life my spouse had forbidden me to expose personal and family issues. My basic beliefs had become, "I have to feel loved by someone else to survive and be happy," or "I have to make this work." I did not yet understand that exploring my beliefs would help me find freedom from my past and begin to heal the wounds that had kept me stuck. I had never counted on anyone but myself, yet I knew I would need some help to unlock the past and step into my future.

The first time I sought out professional help, I felt like I was betraying my family. Like if I needed help, it must mean that something was wrong with me—or my worst fear, that I must be crazy like my older sisters. Revealing my personal history to a stranger felt similar to jumping off a cliff. But each time I left my counseling sessions, my gut told me I would be back, and I sensed a strong desire within me to move forward.

After years as a psychotherapist, I know I need to begin to explore what I am feeling in an emotionally safe place where I can sit and tell my story. A place where I can know that what I say will be kept confidential and that I will not be criticized or judged. Through finding and joining together in this environment I found safety, because a kind of magic took place when I shared my story. In that space I learned to believe in myself and the potential I possess as a woman; my own power and creativity were waiting right inside of me to help change my life. With some encouragement and guidance, I learned to discover my own answers for how to transform my life. Through reaching out in faith, I went on to create a better future.

When faced with decisions, I had always wanted the

path of least resistance. I did my utmost to steer clear of breaking the old rules in my head, and that would include trying something new and uncomfortable. I questioned why I should take the chance of setting myself up for possible failure. Yet what I have discovered since then is when I continue to resist change, it is at the cost of my own joy. I now see my resistance to change can cause me to lose what is mine to claim. I see that through taking action, even though it may be uncomfortable and awkward at first, I grow. Resisting change only prolongs my suffering.

Throughout this book, I include stories of how I found a way to experience life and living in a new way. How, over time, I learned to be grateful for all the things that have happened to me. For, through this dynamic experience, I continue to open my eyes as if for the first time after a long sleep. That is how each day I discover and embrace finding the joy of living my life and understanding that each experience is a masterpiece of God's design.

The Unfolding of a Life

Like the rose she unfolds
Each petal opening gently into another
Revealing new life
Setting herself free
To become

CHAPTER ONE:
THE UNFOLDING

When I was eight years old, my girlfriend and I decided to run away from home. When I look back, it is hard to imagine two eight year olds wanting to leave home. After all, home is where you feel safe when you are eight isn't it? Isn't home a place you want to be?

At this young age, we both knew something was missing in our homes because we talked about leaving them all the time. She lived in her grandparents' house across the street and seldom saw her mom and dad. Together they lived in the old farmhouse with one of her uncles, whom I knew stayed in his room most of the time. Old, worn furniture, musty air, family pictures, and remnants of their family history filled the living room. The garage behind the house held old abandoned cars and tools gathering dust.

Her grandmother would leave pieces of crisp bacon

out on the counter for us when I would come over in the mornings to play. Her words were kind and she was good to my friend. We spent our days outside with our horses and dogs.

What I don't recall is spending much time alone with either of my parents. I needed time with them to learn how I fit in the world, but through most of my childhood years, I was left to figure life out on my own. Being next to youngest in a family with three other sisters, each of us four years apart, I watched my mother constantly running in several directions. There were holes in my life I didn't know how to fill, and I needed a way to bring the gaps together. I longed for someone to share stories with me and help me understand the wonders of the world.

But things were always in a spin in our home with the four of us each having different needs. My dad worked a lot and my mother was too busy for me. From the outside, our family would appear to have everything. A nice home, horses in the pasture behind the house, a boat moored on the river, new cars. We had all the trimmings of a "happy family," yet just under the surface things were about to unravel.

And so, on a nice day, a sunny day, a day my family always attended the annual elementary school picnic, we chose to leave. We knew during all the activities, everyone would be busy having fun and it would take them a while to realize we were gone. Our strategy was to pack up some things and walk to my aunt and uncle's cabin (which was at least an hour or more away by car in the Blue Mountains). We thought we could stay there and then, well…we would just figure out what to do next. That was about the extent of our plan.

After walking home, we set out with only a few things to eat and some clothes thrown into a blanket. Since we lived on the edge of town, it didn't take long until we were on a country road. As it started to get dark, we decided to camp out in a large ditch by the side of the road for the night. We lay on our blanket, listening to the eerie howls of coyotes in the fields around us, scared to death, refusing to go back. We had some matches—part of our survival kit—and began to light a few pieces of paper to keep our hands warm when headlights fell across us.

This was when my father's close friend, a police officer by the name of Alex, driving through the area, spotted our small flames. He was part of what we would later learn was a large rescue party to find us. When he got out of his car, I was relieved to see his familiar face greeting us instead of what I feared, a scary stranger.

His gentle voice calmed us as he helped us pack up our things and loaded us into his shiny black car. I must admit we were a bit relieved at first, but as I climbed in the car, fear gripped me and as we headed for home, my heart started to sink. Thoughts raced through my head about what would happen when I got there. As he drove down the street to our house, we could see cars lining both sides of the road along the way. Many of our neighbors and friends stood in the yards of the homes nearby. I remember how amazed I felt when I realized all these people were looking for us! Up until then, it hadn't occurred to me that two little girls could impact so many other people and their lives. Later I heard the stories of how afraid they all had been that something awful had happened to us, but all I could think about was what my dad would do when I got home.

When we made our plans to run away, all I hoped for was to find a place where I could begin to sense a feeling that I belonged somewhere. I could picture myself in my aunt and uncle's log cabin, a warm wood fire, and breakfast cooking for us, with someone to sit and read to us and spend time with us. But at home, I just felt alone.

Driving into our neighborhood, I had no idea there could ever be any relief for my low sense of worth or any compassion for this little girl who just yearned for love.

What I didn't know was that during this time of my life, my oldest sister, who was in high school, was beginning to exhibit early stages of bipolar disorder. At the same time, my younger sister needed several surgeries to correct a problem with one of her eyes. At eight, you don't have a concept of how these issues affect your parents and how little time my family had to interact with me. Now I understand how this would have put a strain on them and why my parents were barely coping. But then, I had no concept of what was going on. All I knew was I needed to figure out how to take care of myself on my own and there was a deep loneliness in my life. I was fortunate to have girlfriends in the neighborhood, and I remember spending much of my time at their homes and very little time in mine.

At eight years old, it is hard to see the big picture of how your life impacts others. I do remember catching a glimpse of it when Alex brought us home that night. I felt embarrassed, ashamed, and scared. But in the moments after I climbed out of that police car, I only felt a numbing fear. My father's unpredictability, anger, and rage created an atmosphere where emotional safety was hard to come by. When I saw all the people around our home, I knew that, because of all the attention drawn to our family, I would be in trouble for creating a problem. As my mother opened the door, I was crying hysterically, and begged her to not let Dad spank me. Visibly shaken and tired, she put me to bed that night.

I never ran away from home again, but inside my head, where no one could see me, I learned to use this same "running away strategy" over and over again to deal with my emotions. It became easier for me to internally leave myself after that event. It served as a coping strategy in my life, one that would be hard to shake.

Not Knowing Myself

IT STILL SEEMS STRANGE THAT I COULD GO THROUGH SO many years of my life not knowing myself. I longed to understand why there was a voice inside of me that wanted me to punish myself if I made a mistake. That voice told me to be good, not to cause any trouble, and to please others at all cost. I longed to feel good about myself and believe I could possess a sense of worth and value. Yet I believed I had to stick to and live by what was expected of me—or what I perceived was expected. I felt like a boat on the water, adrift. For many reasons, I could not imagine how I would ever get what I needed to feel better about myself. In my head, I stayed hidden in that ditch at the side of the road feeling alone and fearful for many years.

It took a long time and a series of events before I began to see that the beliefs I owned could not change because I wouldn't let them. They couldn't change because I felt a powerful drive within me to keep everything the same. It was the only way I knew how to hold my world together, and I was afraid that if I rocked the boat, did anything differently, things would fall apart. I had learned to keep everything together to prevent my worst fear from happening: being exposed and blamed for failing, because it would be my entire fault, and being punished. I began to live within a rigid sense of unforgiving expectations for myself.

As I listened to this critical voice within me, I established the belief that if I just tried harder things would all work out. If I could just do everything right, everything would be OK. It was like living my life with a broken arm. I needed a cast to help heal my arm and make the pain go away. All I needed to do was get help for my broken arm. But the voice I was listening to wouldn't let me. It was a harsh taskmaster, one that would not allow me to make mistakes or ask for help. Relief was right in front of me all along, but I could not see it or reach out for it. I could not ask for what I needed because, in my core beliefs, I felt I didn't deserve it.

Over the years, I began to become aware that as long as I neglected dealing with my feelings and what wasn't working in my life, everything just got worse. It was like there was a game going on, but I was always on the sidelines, just watching and wishing I could join. As long as I insisted on my position, I was miserable. In time, I found myself out of sync with life and unaware of what could be mine for the asking. I kept refusing to get help for years because my inner voice kept telling me my needs were not important, that I didn't deserve help, and that I needed to maintain my position in the outfield to be safe. No matter what, I just had to keep going and not give up. And I did…till I couldn't anymore.

I knew there was another voice inside of me, waiting,

wanting, trying to be heard. I knew somehow the other voice believed she might find a safe place to be, that place I dreamed of as a little girl, and hidden beneath all of my behaviors, I knew that voice wanted me to change. She kept nudging me, but I kept ignoring her. There was something I had yet to discover.

It takes a long time for a rose bush to bloom. It goes through harsh winters and brutal pruning in the spring. Yet it is in the pruning that the rose bush is set free to unfold. I understand now that, like the rose bush, I went through some difficult times for a reason. I needed to learn things in life I never would have learned without the process of growth.

I am blooming now and as I write, I am claiming the affirmations that lived in me all these years. They are the affirmations of that other voice, the one I spent so much time ignoring but that I can hear now. This voice speaks to me in soft, gentle tones. This voice is not harsh, judgmental, critical, demanding, intolerant, and angry. It brings me out of the darkness and into the light of new awareness, where I find a different way to live. This voice inside of me is learning how to unfold.

A New Heart

Implant within me a new heart
For this one is broken
Permeate the darkness with compassion
So I can see a way
Back to the life I thought I knew

CHAPTER TWO: A NEW HEART

As an adult, learning to give gentle compassion to myself is an ongoing process. Sometimes I still get discouraged and find myself feeling like I just took a huge step backward. It has taken years to create change in my life, yet the rewards are more than worth the effort to get myself moving in a better direction. I worked hard to have an awareness of my feelings and emotions because I wanted to find new ways to deal with the losses in my life. I felt a strong desire to learn how to create balance instead of chaos, and I longed for a life where I could feel whole and sense joy in my heart again.

Old beliefs come up and trip me now and then. They seem to like to catch me when I least expect them. Many are based on experiences from my childhood, when I possessed little control over my environment. Old scenes can keep us from moving forward, or they can serve to help us grow into our adulthood and propel us into a better life. A particular event stands out in my memory.

It happened when I first began to experience how life could feel out of control.

THE HOUSE OF CARDS

AS A KID, I COULDN'T UNDERSTAND MUCH ABOUT MY parents' experiences and what they were going through. I assumed my parents were pretty much omnipotent. I believed this until one night when I was faced with the fact that they weren't.

It happened when I was about ten years old, during a road trip. I wasn't quite sure where we were going, but I knew my parents were tense and I could sense something was wrong. What I didn't know was that life as I knew it would change that night.

It was late and my family was tired when we parked in front of a place called Medical Lake. I didn't know why we were there, but I realized some dreaded thing was about to happen. My parents' silence was palpable and I could feel their discomfort mounting as we sat in the dark car, staring at the foreboding, ominous-looking building in front of us. I overheard them saying something about my sister Judy being in there but I had no idea as why.

I had anticipated seeing something quite different before we arrived at Medical Lake. At my age, the only places I knew that included the word lake in them were wonderful places where my family of six shared fond memories of time spent together waterskiing, swimming, and fishing. Vacations at resorts in the summer every year were great highlights in my life. I had been hanging onto a magical wish that this lake would be like the one in my memories and make things better.

In the past, during the winter months, my whole family would relive these vacation experiences again and again though our home movies. It took incredible patience to wait while Dad cursed and fumed, threading the film into the reels of his treasured eight-millimeter projector. We all knew whenever the feed failed to project the picture right side up the first time, the whole process would need to be repeated, with Dad fuming and fussing all over again. But as soon as the pictures stretched across the white screen, our eyes would fill with delight and paradise returned. Even through the most difficult times, these pictures brought laughter and joy to all of us as they transported us back to the past we longed for.

Now, parked in front of this huge, dark, mental institution with bars on the windows, I saw nothing that matched with my memories. As we waited with our dad in the darkness, I stared through the tears flooding my eyes, longing for my mother to come back out of those massive doors.

As young as I was, I knew just enough to know that people behind bars were there because they were being punished. I possessed no ability to make sense of why Judy was there. I knew she was mixed up, but it wasn't possible for her to be punished. She was a delight to my life and the sister who cared about me and always helped me when I was hurt or sad. She was the compassionate and caring one. The one Mom and Dad adored, as she filled our house with Mozart, Beethoven, and Chopin. Music flowed from her being and wove our hearts together. As my sisters and I would lay under the piano to feel the music or stand behind her, singing carols at Christmas time, we breathed in the one way our family could connect. Her music captured all of us and in its power we felt hope to believe we could rise above anything.

Judy was an accomplished pianist and my parents' pride and joy. At the time she held a scholarship to the Juilliard School of Music. Mom and Dad always believed she held a promising future. She was very much like our Dad, in that she was tall, dark haired, and attractive and had blue eyes. She was close to him and we all knew their relationship was different.

Her behavior started to shift in her late teens, and she would switch back and forth from reserved and shy to grandiose and provocative, common symptoms of the onset of bipolar disorder. It was a great loss to all of us when we recognized that my sister was changing. In our own way we all grieved over the loss of how she had been before.

But how could it be that now she was in this horrid

place that looked like a prison? How could it be that my mother and father knew she was there? And how could it be that I was here, waiting in the dark, desperately wishing with all my heart that she would come out and be with us again? I ached to go back to listening to her play the piano or to the lake we all knew. To run with her on the beach and feel the sun on our faces somewhere we could forget about all this and believe it never happened. It was at this moment, parked in the darkness, that I knew life would never be the same.

A Family Illness

LATER IN MY LIFE, I WOULD COME TO KNOW MY SISTER was being treated for a disorder, which at the time was called manic depression. I knew there was a point where something was different about Judy, and I could recall that, in the year prior to her hospitalization, my parents frequently had arguments about things going on in her life. I also noticed they pored over bills and financial records at our formal dining table. This was in stark contrast to my experience of the past, for, at one time, the table had been used to host family celebrations and elegant dinner parties. My memories of this table, once adorned with beautiful china, silver, and crystal, would be ones that never returned. Now, piles of bills and hours of tension and conflict between my parents led to feelings of trepidation in the house. My sisters and I began to withdraw and stay in our rooms as much as possible.

And so it was that, at this moment, parked in the darkness, I began to experience a dramatic shift in my life. For I knew our family was about to unravel and everything familiar to us was about to change, and I also knew no one was going to talk about what was going on, at least not so I could understand it.

At the time, my parents were trying to protect me by not telling me the truth. In those days, mental illness was little understood. Medications and treatment for my sister's disorder were hard to find. I can rationalize that they believed I would not be able to understand if they tried to explain what was happening. But what they did not know was that I had a desperate need for someone to help me make sense of what became a terrifying maze. It was unfortunate that in their trying to shield me, it only intensified the internalization of my fear and shame.

EVERYTHING IS FINE

IN FRONT OF OTHERS, WE PRETENDED EVERYTHING WAS fine in our house. We continued to go about our lives hiding behind secrets, or at least what we pretended to be. I came to the logical conclusion that if I didn't talk about, it everything would just go away. What I could not foresee at the time was how these childhood beliefs would turn into a way of life and that I would live them out for many years. At the time, all I could feel was ashamed, abandoned, and scared.

In the span of the next eight years, I watched our family collapse as the symptoms of this disorder increased. For not only was my oldest sister, Judy, affected; later, Becky, who was four years younger, would also begin to live out the symptoms of the disorder.

As a parent now, I hold deep compassion for what my own parents went through. In the next few years, my father became more frustrated and angry about what was happening. As Becky's disorder began to manifest itself through her unpredictable behavior and disrespect for any rules, Dad became more frustrated and irritable. I think he saw her as a defiant teen and did not recognize that even though her behavior was different than Judy's, it was still bipolar disorder. Later a psychiatrist added a diagnosis of personality disorder as well. As time went by, Dad became unable to tolerate her actions and resorted to physical and verbal abuse toward her. This only served to increase her symptoms, and I remember countless nights of feeling afraid and helpless when I could only sit and watch in terror while my father beat my sister Becky.

As his anger and intolerance grew, my younger sister Lynn and I lived in fear; his rage would explode at the slightest provocation. As the years went by, I retreated, becoming more repressed and fearful. One day, when my mother was gone and I was home alone with my dad, he became enraged about something and hit me. I recall being shocked that he would do this, because he had never done it before. I fell to the floor and he began to kick me. Somehow I managed to get up and run to my grandparents' house for help. I told them I would never go back home.

When my mother came to my grandparents' home, we sat at the kitchen table and she promised me she had talked with my dad and it would never happen again. Though reluctant, I returned home, and although he never beat me again, I still witnessed my older sister Becky's abuse. It took years of professional therapy to forgive myself for not being able to know how to stop him from hurting her. I needed to recognize I was just a little girl at the time and there was no way I could have stopped him.

With no self-esteem or confidence in myself, I began making decisions based on little hope for my future. My body could not cope well with the ongoing stress, and I began to get sick with an upset stomach, not want to go to school, and experience light-headedness and fatigue.

WHAT I KNOW NOW

LIKE MANY OF THE WOMEN I SEE TODAY, I GREW UP BE-lieving there was little in this world for me. That whatever I could manage to hang onto would be all I could expect. I learned to not hope for my dreams to come true, and came to see the world as a place where love was hard to find and where there was little for me.

What I was yet to discover were the wonderful people who would and could be there for me. The hardships I suffered were difficult, but I did not give up, and with the help of others, I came to recognize how to not repeat my history. I learned how to find a way back into the light.

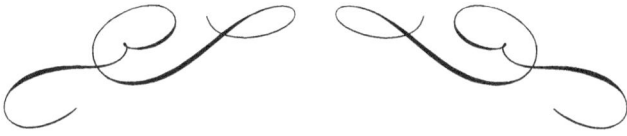

In the Garden

He meets me in the garden
Mixed among the rows of green
Greets me with his gentle eyes
And suddenly I'm seen

CHAPTER THREE: THE GARDEN OF EMPATHY

In my mind's eye, I can still see the rolling wheat fields that surround the small town where I grew up. They have the most radiant golden color as they enter harvest time and burst full in the hot sun of those summer months. The gentle acres surrounding the town were abundant with a variety of grains. Many times, as I walked or rode my horse near the fields, I would hear the sudden burst of a pheasant's wings pushing through the stalks of grain and taking it into flight.

My grandfather, who once made a living by farming the wheat and raising racehorses, was in his retirement and lived near us. A large garden separated our house from my grandparents' home, and Grandfather spent summers in the garden, where he raised every vegetable one could imagine. He would work endless hours tending it for our families to use. I could see how hard he worked, and knew it was a labor of love and a gift to all of us. He wore a wide-brimmed felt hat, and a large cotton handkerchief hung from the pocket of his bib overalls. I can still see the metal hooks holding them up on his shoulders.

I knew if he wasn't in the garden I could find him sitting in the kitchen with Grandmother and my uncle Wes, who lived with them. Grandpa was a huge baseball fan, and sometimes he would be in the living room watching the games. But in the summer when I came over to see him, Grandpa would often be coming up the garden path from the barn behind their home, where he cared for the milk cows, pigs, and chickens. Hot from the sun, he would pull his handkerchief from his pocket and wipe his brow along the way.

What I remember the most about him is the smile he would greet me with. When I saw him smile, it felt like all his love just wrapped around my heart. When his eyes met with mine, I knew that between us there was a sense of deep heartfelt connection; he was always ready to listen to even my smallest need. Without a doubt, I knew he loved and accepted me—just for me. I wish now I could tell him how his presence was such a blessing. His ability to have empathy and concern for me christened me with a sense of my own existence. His existence and presence provided safety and hope in the midst of my life. It was as if Grandpa's gentle reassurance resonated in me through the natural orchestration of his breath, movements, smell, touch, and voice. All of his rich character and value still collide in my mind to help me relive the relationship we knew.

He helped me gain a sense of who I was in the world. He represented emotional shelter for me, through his tenderness and compassion. My sense of him is sweet and I cherish recalling the scent of horse liniment and his large hands rubbing it against my bay mare's lame front tendons. Grandfather loved horses, and with his encouragement, when I was still very young, I rode my own horse on the trails near where we all lived, on the edge of town.

My moments in the garden with him still give me hope today as I acknowledge the anchor he was in my life. His presence, support, and loving kindness bestow me with resilience when the storms of life threaten.

None to Be Found

AT HOME, NEITHER OF MY PARENTS HAD THE TIME TO come sit by my bed or talk about how my day went. I was hard pressed to find a safe place to share my struggles, feelings, or simple needs of the day. At home, I became lonely and introverted. I needed my parents to reflect my feelings back and help me sort out who I was inside.

Up until I entered middle school, my parents were able to keep their marriage together. When both my sisters became bipolar and the financial and emotional stress became too great, my parents separated. My mother moved away to our summer house on Puget Sound. None of us girls went with her.

What surrounded her decision to leave us was never clear to me. I could only try to piece things together and go on. It all seemed like a disconnected nightmare, into which our lives were disappearing. I knew something was desperately wrong and I heard bits and pieces of conversations about my mother being hospitalized for a brief period of time in another town. Friends said my mother was acting strange, and I felt a sense of shame as well as confusion about to why they would say this to me. All I knew was that I loved my mother and that things were definitely changing in our home.

We continued to live in our same house, and Dad hired a nanny to care for us. The nanny stayed in a bedroom near mine. It was good to have someone there when I came home from school. The wondrous smell filling the house, of fresh bread and rolls, when I walked in the door brought me a sense of comfort. She was a great cook and prepared our meals and did our laundry, and we went on the best we could.

As time went by, money became tight and Dad sold the only home I ever knew. I was sent to live with Aunt Wilma and Uncle Ed, who lived next to my grandparents' home in a very small, old house. I remember they had a wood stove in the kitchen that they brought firewood in for. I had to share a bedroom with my cousin Fred, who was a few years older than me. I was just going into puberty at the time, and the strangeness of living in a room with a male was completely foreign to me. Their house was much older and smaller than ours, and we all shared the same bathroom. They lived a very different lifestyle than I the one I had known, and everything I experienced there was different than what I knew. I do remember that they were kind to me. I felt uncomfortable and confused about why I was put into this position, but did not question what was handed to me. My world and my life were falling apart, and I realized I would need to accept anything I could get. It was as if the earth had crumbled beneath my feet and any sense of stability I ever knew was gone.

When I allow myself to experience the memories of staying in the room with Fred, I feel my internal sense of control slip away from me. At the time, I could not comprehend how destructive this experience was, but when I think of this today, an intense sense of desolation wells up within my body.

What troubled me also was that my dad and Lynn, my youngest sister, lived with my mother's parents. I thought it was strange that my dad would live with my mother's parents. I never saw my dad much when I lived in my aunt and uncle's house. I was very young, and I know there are bits and pieces I will never know, but the secrets of those times and what happened to us is a sad legacy. When I think back to my experience, it is like seeing myself walking up to a curtain. I want to know what is behind it, but when I start to pull the curtain back, I can't. Today I know I don't have to see what was there. My body remembers the trauma, and as an adult, I can help old wounds heal through giving myself the very things I didn't get back then: peace, health, and safety.

What I do know is I got through it, and acknowledging today what happened to me then helps explain so much about my fears, behaviors, and beliefs in the past. It helps me see how I developed my relationships with men and why I felt helpless through my teens and young adulthood when it came to constructing boundaries for myself. I am so grateful for my grandfather and his model of empathy that served as an example of hope. His model leads me back to a place of grace in the Garden of Empathy after all these years.

Someone Else's Life

Always second-guessing
Reading others' minds
Help me to recognize
This life I live is mine

CHAPTER FOUR: ROLES
AND SCRIPTS

In my office, I have a picture of my mother sitting on a racehorse. I would guess she is in her late teens or early twenties in the photo. She is riding in front of a large grandstand predominately full of men. My beloved grandfather, who at the time was a wheat rancher, also raised thoroughbred racehorses and owned the incredible thoroughbred she is astride. Back then, my mother rode for my grandfather at many of the famous racetracks throughout the Northwest. I keep her picture there to remind me of what I admired the most in her. Her petite body is dwarfed in size by her mount; yet she sits fearless and erect in the saddle. Her posture is that of a strong woman who knows who she is and where she is going. As I look at her, I see someone who found and held her true passion firmly in the reins of a powerful racehorse. Her face depicts sheer determination, intention, presence, direction, faith, and confidence. These are the qualities

I know my mother held when she rode horses, and her history as a rider affirms them. I strive to model much of who I am after her image in that picture.

I can still hear her telling me the stories of how people would pay her a hundred dollars just so they could see her ride around the track. Today I would pay a million to see her in that part of her life again. That was when she was offered a future at Madison Square Garden to demonstrate her riding talent. She gave all that up to have a family because, back then, that was what women did. Her sacrifice turned out to be far greater than the demands of any thoroughbred racehorse could have been.

FAMILY ROLES: THE CAST

EVERY FAMILY HAS ESTABLISHED ROLES FOR EACH MEMber, and in my family of origin, I knew which one belonged to me. The rules associated with my role were, Be good, look good, don't make any trouble, keep a low profile. and for God's sake, do everything you possibly can to make everyone happy—and do not, under any circumstances, piss Dad off. What I didn't know, and could not have known, was that with a father who acted out all the behaviors of an undiagnosed bipolar and a mother who was incredibly passive, the stage was perfectly set for a performance with a sad ending.

As a child, I came to know my family's implicit message about how to fit in and please everyone. So I quickly figured out that the purpose of my behavior was all about performance. I became driven to find out how much I could do to earn attention and love. I would go to great lengths to accomplish this end. But at our family table, I learned that I didn't deserve to be noticed, affirmed, or valued. Life was about performance, and I didn't shine in that scene. What unfolded in the scenes of our family dinners would work to make me believe I needed to be someone other than me. I learned how not to believe in myself, to doubt my value and worth, and to make desperate attempts to interpret the chaos so I could fit in. All of us played out our roles as they unfolded through the scenes at our kitchen table.

THE DINNER TABLE, ACT I: THE PREPARATION

IT USUALLY STARTED WITH DAD'S ARRIVAL HOME FROM work. We four girls knew how the stage would be set for the first act. The correct preparation for Dad coming home for dinner was crucial, because it set the stage. As the time came for him to arrive, the whole mood of the house began to shift. It was like a switch was thrown, and it was followed by each of us taking on our part of the script and acting it out.

Prior to his arrival, each of us helped prepare dinner, set the table, and get to our places. The camera was turned on and we became actors on a stage. Dad's slippers were brought out, the table was prepared and his newspaper placed in a special stand with a place setting just for him. Dinner was always ready and we were all in our proper places, on cue and ready for the performance.

ACT II: SEATING ARRANGEMENT

IN OUR HOME, A LARGE RECTANGULAR ISLAND SEPA-rated the kitchen from the family room. With my two older sisters, I always sat on the family-room side. My dad sat directly across from me, on the other side of the island, with my mother next to him and my youngest sister, Lynn, on the end by Mom. These seating assignments created the perfect setup for the scenes that would be played out time after time, and each sister's position served to anchor us in our roles.

My oldest sister Judy, whose role was firmly established as the perfect child, typically served as the focus of attention. Judy was eight years older than I; she sat on my right. Judy and Dad connected on every level. Both were very competitive and loved to challenge each other. She was given a beautiful baby grand piano and the best piano instruction, and knew how to perform. Judy, whose incredible talent became evident early in her life, drew Dad close to her and he adored her and her talent. It was as if they melded into each other when they were together. He would sit for hours, listening to her play music from every era and style. She could play jazz, classical, spiritual—whatever he desired her to play. She learned well how to please him with the old songs he loved and held him mesmerized with her style of musical arrangements. They would also spar and compete for each other's attentions, and it was clear through the years that Judy was his favorite. Little did he know then that she would also become his perfect storm when, later, in her teens, she would become bipolar and for years lose her ability to perform. His dream that she would someday be a concert pianist vanished.

Act III: Calm Down, Jim!

AS THE YEARS PASSED, BECKY, WHO SAT ON THE OTHER end of the kitchen island, became a scapegoat for Dad's anger as his disappointment regarding Judy's mental health was exacerbated by Becky's clear defiance of him. His inability to deal with the devastation of Judy's mental health created an irritability that pervaded the scenes of our lives. Judy spent the next several years in and out of treatment facilities, and by the time she was out of high school, she had entered the revolving doors of mental institutions and hospitals.

After Judy left home, I sat directly across from Dad at the dinner table. Things would start out with Dad setting the mood. He would typically start by targeting Becky (the scapegoat) regarding what she did wrong that day. Since I sat directly across from him, I got a firsthand read of his body language and would be the first to see what was coming. Dad would start to get mad at Becky, and Mom would begin to placate him and try to get him to calm down.

My mother's role was very complicated for me. In some ways she appeared so strong and confident, and yet when it came to my dad, we all knew who ruled the house. I do not remember my mother ever having a conflict with him in front of us or trying to stop him from being so demanding and mean to us. It was clear she wanted to appease him when he got angry and I remember the phrase she used over and over, "Calm down Jim." Invariably this preceded all hell breaking loose, and I would watch Dad's jaw set, the veins in his neck pop out, and his face contort. He would rise out of his chair and come around behind me to go to the other end of the island to where Becky—always seated the farthest away from him—would be. He would grab her by the hair and fling her to the other end of the room—so appropriately named "the family room"—as the rest of us sat watching, terrified of what would happen next. In those moments, my mother all but disappeared. We were left to fend for ourselves. I often wondered why.

My youngest sister Lynn, the invisible child, sat in clear view of this scene unfolding, as she sat directly opposite Becky. Since she was very young at that time, it is little wonder that today she remembers none of her childhood. When I think about her witnessing what she saw, I cannot begin to dream of how terrifying it would have been for a little girl. It is no wonder she and I grew up to believe we were helpless victims instead of learning to trust or get close to anyone.

It took years for me to comprehend the outliers of these scenes, to recognize that observing Becky's victimization served to make Lynn and me into vicarious victims of verbal and physical assault and abuse. This left us in a conflicted role that led to long-term consequences for both of us. Our roles became complex, as we carried guilt for feeling relieved that we were not being beaten. It proved to be a very complicated script to understand.

THE WRITING OF A SCRIPT

THE FAMILY ROLES WE TOOK ON IN OUR CHILDHOOD proved to be the unfortunate outcome of the Act III. For because of this act, we carried what we learned as children into the roles of our adult lives. Each of us struggled for many years to try and change the legacy of our scripted lives. It took years for us to sort out how entrenched these roles were and how practicing and acting out our parts over and over again had led us to believe that those scripts were "normal" and expected. For many years, I could not understand the effects of what my sisters and I suffered. I knew what we went through felt horrible, and I knew the internalized sense of shame and sadness the roles created for all of us, but I had yet to see how we all tried so hard to make the scripts we were given work.

OFF TO CHURCH

I DIDN'T ASK ANY QUESTIONS, BECAUSE I KNEW I WOULD not get answers. Questions and answers in my family were avoided, along with truth telling, which led to constant chaos and drama. So while we all attended church on Sundays, we left ourselves behind at home. No one would have recognized our internal sadness and shame when they saw us sitting in the pew. Each of us knew living in our house was like looking into the distorted mirrors at the circus. We became masters at putting on the image others expected, because we all memorized and knew our roles well.

I just wanted to fit in and not feel so alone. So part of playing my role was learning how to make myself disappear on a physical and emotional level. I made desperate attempts to fade into the background so as not to be noticed, because things just seemed more bearable when I wasn't seen. For the most part, Lynn and I found that being invisible kept us under Dad's radar, and as Judy and Becky demanded more of his attention, this became easier to do. We would both spend most of our time off with friends where we could get a sense of a family.

THE LAST ACT

LYNN AND I LEARNED SOME IMPLICIT LESSONS THROUGHout our childhood. For the most part, we learned it was about what you do and how you look, not who you are. So we spent a lot of time living out trying to be someone other than who we were. We also learned to just survive and get through it, interpret what was going on the best we could, and try to fit in and make everything work. For a kid, doing this takes a huge amount of energy and does little to help develop personal growth or cultivate trust. As a result, neither of us ever talked about our hopes for the future. We doubted ourselves and didn't trust others. Just getting through what was happening in our home was the best we could do. I don't remember ever being asked what I wanted to be when I grew up. For me, college was never spoken of, nor any of my dreams cultivated. I was ill equipped to step out into the world as a young adult, and as a result made choices based on what I believed was all I had.

It is fortunate for me that my mother also gave me a gift I could not have lived without: faith. I am grateful that today I can claim the qualities in my mother that helped to sustain and encourage me in my own personal growth. Her determination, intention, presence, direction, faith, and confidence endure through my life as I learn to transform and re-create myself. Her qualities endure in and through the picture I hold of her when her life was full of passion. I am moving forward to reframe my life and rewrite the old scripts once handed down to me. I now know I can choose to live in the freedom of my own internal spirit, where the voice that speaks to me resonates with courage, trust, and hope.

Our Meeting

Love seems to seek itself
Goes beyond the edge and reaches farther
Wants for what most would only dream
And then stretches harder

For only then can it breathe
When the soul meets its match
And finds the joy
Love can only know as it's own

CHAPTER FIVE: LOST

"When one is a stranger to oneself, then one is estranged from others too. If one is out of touch with oneself, then one cannot touch others."

—ANNE MORROW LINDBERGH

At one point during my parents' separation, my dad took us on a trip to see Mom at the house a few miles outside Sequim, Washington. Originally built of their shared dreams, the house sat atop a hill, surrounded by vast fields of rich emerald-green alfalfa. When we drove up, it stood alone as if holding sentinel over the land, which sloped gently down to meet coastal homes and a natural spit that extended far out into the ocean to greet the Strait of Juan de Fuca. On the very tip stood a lighthouse holding the beacon for vast cargo ships and freighters making their way through the straits.

In the years before my parents' separation, we had

visited several times as they worked to plan and build the summerhouse. At one time, I knew it held the visions of what was to be their future. My mother and father always loved the water, and Dad was an avid fisherman. It seemed the perfect place for them to retire someday. At night, we would sit in front of the natural stone fireplace and look off in the distance, delighting at the sparkling lights of Victoria, Canada. I have fond memories of when Mother and I would wander the beach, laden with driftwood and prized finds of treasured glass floats lost from fishermen's nets.

When we arrived to visit after the separation, it was so good to see Mom again, and yet she seemed so different and everything about her felt surreal. I was aware that she had had some kind of a breakdown in the last year and tried not to expect too much of her. She told us she was working in a department store not too far away, in another town called Port Angeles. For her to have a job seemed so foreign to me, since in my lifetime I had never known her to work outside of our home. After all our time apart, it felt strange to be in a different house with her, and yet at the same time wonderful to be together again. She went out of her way to welcome us and make special meals and treats. She tried to shower us with the attention we so yearned for, but experiencing it felt awkward and unnatural. In the years past, Mom had not been emotionally connected with us, and there was nothing to hang on to. No soft hands held ours, no tender kisses on our heads or gentle strokes to fall across our heads or to tuck our hair behind our ears. For her to act so caring was confusing and strange. We didn't know how to accept her emotional and physical closeness or figure out how to respond to her unfamiliar attentiveness.

So it came with a mixture of emotions when Dad decided it was time to leave. In my mind's eye, I can still see my mother standing outside my passenger car window crying and begging Lynn and me to stay. Those memories are etched deep within me alongside the tears that streamed down my face. My heart felt so torn between life with my mother and life without her.

Over the next months, my parents decided to get back together, and Dad moved us to the summerhouse near Sequim to live. By this time, Becky was in college, and Lynn and I found ourselves leaving our hometown to start new schools. It was like having an out-of-body experience when I walked into the classroom there. Starting school in the middle of a term felt like moving to a foreign country. I did not know how to integrate with the other students, and knew they were used to their own routine of friends and activities. Back home, I would have known nearly everyone in my school. Life there seemed more natural; I had grown up with so many familiar people and places—yet here, when I walked into the classroom, the kids stared at me and whispered to each other. I felt exposed and vulnerable. As a young adolescent girl, merging into a new school was awful, and it seemed impossible for me to find my way.

The move back to the summerhouse was difficult. The only thing that kept me going was that we could take my horse, Latassa, with us. She had been the one constant in my life throughout the time of my parents' separation, and she represented a huge part of my family's history, handed down by my grandfather and my mother. Up until then, my horse provided a way of life. The activities we did in the community were strongly connected to horses. Latassa gave me something I knew I could hold on to through the emotional storms of my childhood, when my mother abandoned us. Without her, I would have been lost. Some relatives of my mother's agreed to take Lynn and me with them in their car and pull the horse trailer. We took my horse, my beautiful Arabian bay mare, and moved.

Back in our hometown, I grew up riding almost every day. I belonged to a riding group and also did a little racing at the local rodeos. My horse was a delight to ride in parades. She was high-spirited, as Arabians often are, and carried her head high as her tiny hoofs pranced across the pavement, barely touching in stride. We also performed for crowds at the fair with my riding team. She was always there for me and she was my faithful friend who listened to my every complaint. My confidante. In the barn, I would groom her and share all of the day's problems and concerns. The smell of her hair as I ran the brush over her soothed me. Her warm body against my hand brought me comfort. There was a repetition of folding my opposite palm over where the brush just passed and it passed love through me to her and back again. The barn and hay connected me to a sense of solace and belonging. The feel and scent of her leather bridle and saddle, handed down to me from my mother, were cherished gifts.

It was late when we arrived at the house after the move. My parents hadn't had a chance to put a fence in to pasture the horses, so they decided to stake them out in the field near the house. The horses hadn't been staked before, and it seemed strange to me they would not have made some other plans for them. Why we could not just put them back in the horse trailer puzzled me. I kept thinking they would get spooked in the night when wild animals came around. I could not imagine that a stake in the ground could keep them from bolting and breaking free. My worst fear was they would get loose in the night. The next morning the horses were gone.

Several frantic hours later, we received a phone call from a kind couple at a farm nearby. They had found them, and with great relief and excitement we all went together to bring them home. Later, we learned the couple had discovered the two of them that morning and somehow located us through other families in the area. When we arrived, Lynn's Rhone was fine, but my mare had become entangled in a large roll of barbed wire. When horses get into barbed wire, they fight it and only make it worse. The sharp spikes had ripped her entire foreleg and torn it open to the bone. Her whole body was trembling, and she stood there, frozen in shock. To look at her was horrifying. Watching this beautiful creature standing there like that was more than I could endure. I turned and ran to the car so I could not see her. It was too painful.

She lived at the veterinary clinic in town for weeks in the hopes of saving her. It was a long recovery, and she would never be the same. Neither would I. She was my friend and the only one I could tell all my secrets to. Her love for me was unconditional and irreplaceable. The coveted hours I spent riding her daily for consolation had been replaced by visits to the clinic to see her over-medicated for pain and trauma. At the time, I thought my life could not get any darker. I felt such a sense of being out of my control and I felt so lost. Without Latassa, my strength was gone. There would be no consolation for me now, since she had provided a sense of support and hope. It seemed everything I counted on had left.

We lived in Sequim for several months while Latassa recovered. Lynn and I tried to adjust, but we were both miserable there. Living out in the country without our old friends and the town we loved and knew seemed so difficult. It was a huge relief when our parents decided to move back to Walla Walla. We took the horses home, and Latassa returned to her pasture behind the house. It is amazing how horses can heal, and I was so grateful to have her back. My parents had somehow managed to purchase our previous home back, and we were delighted because we longed to have some sense of belonging again. At last we thought things would be okay. Soon I would start high school and be with my friends again.

What I couldn't see then was the big picture of how these experiences were affecting my perceptions of the world. How the constant disruptions of moving and instability created such turmoil for establishing my own visions of a future and dreams of who I could be. The basic tools I would need to create healthy relationships for myself were lost along the way. I did not know how to deal with life, how to make new friends, and how to live a mindset of more than just survival.

I was ill equipped to start my high school years and start to make decisions that would affect the rest of my life. The scars Latassa suffered affected her for the rest of her life, and the wounds I endured as a result of neglect rendered me lost for years to come.

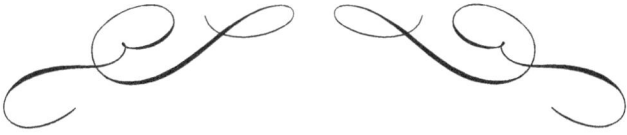

TETHER ME

Tether me to your heart, Lord
That I won't wander off
Forget to seek your face
And live my life without your grace

CHAPTER SIX: SWEET SIXTEEN

By the time I entered high school, any guy who would pay attention to me drew me in like a magnet. I dated a few different guys my sophomore year and then I met the man of my dreams. We were perfect for each other…or so I thought.

I lived for him from that moment on. Nothing else and nobody else could tell me he wasn't who I thought he was because I believed all my dreams had come true. He was handsome, a meticulous dresser, charismatic, tall, intelligent, popular, and OMG…a senior. I was blind to everything and anything that would be important to notice in a relationship. At that time, I didn't know and I didn't care who he was, because he rescued me from the awful emptiness I felt inside and gave me the instant sense of self-esteem and belonging I longed for. I was his girlfriend and I was on top of the world. All that mattered was being with him, and from the very start I would do anything to keep the relationship.

Walking through the teen years of my life was a blur.

It was all about just getting through. At home, no one ever spoke to me about what the future could be or about any possibilities for a college education. The only hope came during a class the first two months of my senior year just before I dropped out.

A history teacher treated me differently. For the first time, someone seemed to believe I was intelligent and could answer questions in class. He encouraged my participation by calling on and including me, openly treating me as if I had something to offer. Because he showed a sincere interest in my education, I started to develop a new sense of awareness of myself in the world.

All this was taking place during the time our country was ramping up for the Vietnam War. The television news flooded our homes every night with horrifying pictures of our young men dying in battle. In my teens, I felt somehow removed from the scenes on the TV. It was as if it was so far away and too hard for me to believe, let alone understand or feel like something I could do anything about. Many people were protesting the war during that time and some were leaving the country at great risk to themselves to seek safety from what they believed would be certain death. Most adults viewed them as traitors to our country. We heard the reports of how millions of gallons of herbicidal warfare were being dropped and affecting enormous numbers of Vietnamese people as well as our troops.

During this time, teen girls in the United States did not realize they were vulnerable casualties of the war as well. I was one of those girls, oblivious as to how this could directly affect me. When I was sixteen, information about how to take care of and protect myself sexually was not provided at home or in the schools. After all, sex was forbidden. No surprise I was exposed to unprotected sex with my future husband countless times before we were married. It wasn't until just after we were married that he would receive the final papers from the government stating he would not be drafted due to my pregnancy and marital status. It didn't hit me until then that I, and the child I was carrying, actually saved his life.

It amazes me how young women were kept in such a place where they did not comprehend the issues of the war. I look back and see myself as one among many who thought they were lucky to have a boyfriend, but unaware of the price. Keeping young girls naive and not giving them information and access to contraception puts them at risk and renders them helpless.

My boyfriend went off to college the next fall, but came back without finishing out the year. We sent letters to each other almost every day when he was gone. When he returned, I could hardly wait to see him. We started dating again, but my parents wanted me to stop, so I tried to break it off for a while. I could see he was starting to hang out with some guys that were considered pretty wild. These were guys who stayed in our hometown instead of going away to college. I wondered about what direction he was going. We would still sneak out to meet each other, but it didn't take long before he was openly dating another girl and I was dating too.

A few weeks into my senior year, I started gaining weight. I was having some irregular menses, so I asked my girlfriend to go with me to see the doctor just to see if I might be pregnant. At the time in history, it was uncommon to talk about intercourse or prevention. My boyfriend and I skirted the topic and the reality of a pregnancy seemed remote. Since we had dated a long time and I had not become pregnant, I was naïve about the idea. The issue of birth control and the use of condoms wasn't something we talked about. Even the idea of being pregnant was difficult for me to face. Over the next two weeks, I had to come to grips with what seemed impossible to believe. The morning sickness I excused as the flu, the weight gain I dismissed as eating too much, the tender breasts…I ignored all of it until I couldn't.

So, two weeks later, with my illusions crumbling, I went back to the doctor and confessed I might be pregnant. He confirmed I was close to four months along. He explained he had wanted to give me time to face what was happening. I appreciated the fact that he respected me enough to allow me to face the inevitable in my own way and time.

In those days, fewer girls considered that there were any options for pregnancy other than marriage, and would not think to explore the idea of adoption or abortion. I saw pregnancy as leaving me little choice but to get married at seventeen, leave my hometown, and move away from everyone and everything I knew. In making the decision to "do the right thing and get married," I became ostracized in the community. Many of my friends' parents would not let their daughters associate with me after they learned I was pregnant.

At first we talked about just going somewhere and getting married, but in the end, decided to tell our parents at the same time that Saturday morning. We planned to tell them separately and see how things went from there.

Building up the courage to tell them was horrifying. I remember struggling about how to do it with my older sister Becky, who was now twenty, and my younger sister, Lynn, now twelve, standing by. The kicker was that Becky was also pregnant at the time, and she wanted us to tell our parents at the same time! In the end she agreed to let me tell them first, since his parents were on their way over to our house to talk about what to do.

My parents and his parents sat together with us, and our parents decided it was best we get married. Within four days, I had picked out a wedding dress, a lovely, brocade, off-white sheath, and a going-away suit, including a hat and gloves. We were actually married in the church our family had always attended with the associate minister presiding and about fifty people attending, including relatives and close friends. I even had a bridesmaid and he had a best man. The local paper announced our wedding and honeymoon plans. Following the wedding, there was even a reception with cake and punch. My mother was the consummate hostess and arranged everything down to the nuts and mints. It was like going through a whirlwind, and then it was over.

In a small town like the one I grew up in, everyone knows what is happening to you. Many of our friends' parents would not let their kids have anything to do with us because it was shameful to be pregnant before you were married. Somehow I think they thought it might be contagious if their kids hung around us. We were considered a bad influence.

So we decided to have the car packed at the end of the ceremony and head out for our honeymoon, which consisted of a one-night stay at a hotel in Portland, Oregon. We would then go stay with a close friend of my husband's. They had spoken on the phone earlier that week. Ben was married, had a job, and was living in Springfield, Oregon. He said we were welcome to come and stay with them until we could find a place. When we arrived, we found they were living in a studio apartment and the refrigerator had nothing in it but a large package of bologna and some sliced cheese. The two of them stayed nights with some friends until we could get settled. Within the next week, his friend helped my husband get a job, find an apartment near the store where he worked—which at that time paid $1.50 and a half cent per hour—and we were set! Or so we thought.

It didn't take long for reality to set in. For the first time in my life, I was by myself all day, facing the enormity of my choices. From that point on, life was about survival. I would be the good wife, just like I was the good kid, and try hard to make it all work. I was desperate for friends, and no one my age lived in the apartment house. One thing I knew for sure was that I could not go back home, no matter how hard things got. With my sister Becky pregnant and having serious problems due to her bipolar disorder, things were not good back home.

At seventeen, I found myself between two worlds: one of being married and pregnant, the other of being a teen who knew nothing of living in an adult world. I felt lost between the two. I had no idea what to do or where to go for help and support. In the 1960s, there were limited services in the community for pregnant teens. But in Springfield there was a night program—which was considered a pioneering program at the time—at the local high school for senior students who needed to finish school. I signed up.

There were about twenty girls in the class, all pregnant, and 99 percent of them were cheerleaders. A former flag twirler from Walla Walla High School, I was the exception. I met a girl there and we became friends. I somehow managed to finish high school, in spite of the fact that we moved back to our hometown a few weeks before I was scheduled to complete.

The supervisor at the night school program offered to help me complete the required courses, coordinating a way for me to complete classes in our hometown. I will always be grateful to her. When I sent proof of my classes later, she sent my diploma. Little did I know it then, but her acts of kindness would help me go back to college one day and eventually finish a master's degree. She will never know how much that meant to me. Years later, just like her, I went on to become a school counselor and eventually started a private practice as a psychotherapist. I can only hope I helped others along the way like she helped me. At that time, I would never have known my education would be the ticket to my future, my personal growth, my ability to learn how to be an adult, and my freedom to discover a passion for my life work.

By the night I would have graduated as a senior with my class in Walla Walla, I was in my hometown, sitting alone on the front steps of our duplex, crying. I was holding a diploma from Springfield High School, even though I technically had never set foot in a regular class there. I could imagine my real graduating class that night, the pride they all felt, what the ceremony would look like, but I could not bring myself to go and watch my friends graduate without me. All my friends, along with a lifetime of memories, would go without celebration. At eighteen years old, I believed my future to be set in concrete. Changing anything would not be an option. I would live out my choices and learn to deal with the emotional pain. It was a very lonely night for me, with no one to celebrate the joy of my accomplishment.

From the beginning, I invested everything in my husband, because I saw him as my identity. My world revolved around what I could do to make him happy, which is hard to do especially when you are unhappy, but I gave it my best. It took me a long time to recognize that investing in someone's happiness or identity was not my job. It was theirs. My job was to invest in me, so I could find out what made me happy and find my own identity. When I look back now, I recognize how very mixed up the world had become for me. Yet I can also look at myself as a young girl who was doing her best and have compassion for her. She just wanted to be loved and accepted and figure out how she fit in the world. But what I learned in my childhood was that I had no control over my own future, no ability or personal power to change my own life. Worse yet, because of the things that happened to me, I believed I did not deserve a better life.

Holding onto the beliefs I held to survive when I was young, despite how they affected my life, did not serve me well as I moved into adulthood. Yet all along there was a series of people who came into my life and helped me to believe in my ability to change. I started to realize that when I neglect my own needs, I hold myself back from living the precious life I have been given. I started to recognize how staying numb for so many years kept me from creating a better life and seeing other ways to live life.

Me Again

Life comes sweetly when it returns
After being so patient for us
To get to know ourself
So we can finally meet

CHAPTER SEVEN:
WHERE ARE YOU?

At eighteen, I was a young mom living in a duplex in Eugene, Oregon, with very little money, no car, and no friends. I spent my days caring for my infant son, Chad. I was just a child myself with little of what I needed to be a parent. It was strange to me that family and friends seemed to expect me to know how to parent without any experience of ever being with an infant. Chad and I just had to figure it out on our own. I guess I was just supposed to know how to care for babies because I had one.

The one person I knew who lived in Eugene was my oldest sister, Judy. She was married with three children of her own and lived several miles away. At times, she would struggle through episodes of mania and depression. So when I would have the car for the day, I could go take care of the kids and clean the house when things were going sideways for her. Entering the house was like walking into a war zone. Every room would be in a complete state of chaos, with piles of laundry and dirty dishes, and Judy would be in bed. The kids needed lots of love and attention, which I was happy to give. The hardest part was when I would find the youngest alone in her crib. Sometimes I just wanted to take her home, because I knew she got so little attention. We all held our breath for Judy to get through the bottom of her depression, which typically came on the tail end of a blow-your-mind high. Her behavior would become so unpredictable and bizarre, it was all any of us could do to wait for the dust to settle. When it did, there were good times and she was able to be a sister to me and a mother to her children. We waited for the storms to blow over so we could all enjoy being together on weekends for dinner, when her husband would make spaghetti, Judy would play the piano, and we could all enjoy being a family. We were all so glad when things got better.

The only other person in my world was an eighty-five-year-old woman in the duplex next to ours. Due to a stroke, she could barely talk and used hand signals to convey her needs. She lived with her daughter who worked during the day. I don't remember her name, but I do remember her smile when on rare sunny days she stood at her back door of the duplex, watching me as I hung diapers on the clothesline. To my delight, sometimes she would signal me to come over. There were a few toys in the closet and she would show me where they were and encourage me to get them so Chad could play. It was a comfort to have someone else show an interest in us, and we enjoyed her presence. I look back now and realize how lonely both of us were and how much her smile and friendship enriched my day.

I did not know how to navigate the world. I was too young to be in the adult world, and having a child put me in a different place than others my age. I wanted to have some money of my own and decided to take in ironing to make enough to shop for some kind of craft at a variety store nearby. I remember it being a big event to put Chad in the stroller and go look at the yarn at the store. I yearned to have something creative to do to pass the time when Chad took his naps. An older woman who worked there befriended me and offered to teach me how to crochet a baby blanket. She invited me to come over on her lunch hour, and together we would sit in her car and she would teach me to crochet while she ate her lunch.

Through people's loving kindness and support, I began to realize there were others in the world that cared about me. I found hope through the compassionate acts of people I met as we moved from town to town. Their kindness provided a way for me to get through those lonely times.

I don't know if either of the women who befriended

me in Eugene knew it, but they were my only friends. Each of them helped me get through those early days of being a wife and mother. At seventeen, there was no way I could have foreseen how getting pregnant would bring such difficult challenges into my life. As a young mother, I was lost as to where or how I fit into the world. I accepted responsibility for the choices I made, but the loneliness turned out to be something more than I bargained for.

As time went by, I started to read again and went back to church, joined an exercise class, and began to meet other young mothers with small children. But just as I would start to get my balance, we would move. We moved over and over again during the thirty-two years of our marriage—thirty-two moves through sixteen towns, as a matter of fact. It became nearly impossible for me to sort things out. Just when I would start to get my feet on the ground, we would move again and I would leave dear friends and the stability I gained in a community. To understand what I needed became elusive; to find a sense of who I was and where I was going on a personal level…next to impossible.

Looking back on myself as a young girl, it is easy for me now to see the reasons for a lot of my pain. Isolated in an apartment, taking care of an infant, did little to support my own development for becoming an adult, wife, and parent. As the years passed and my two other sons were born, I continued to want be home with them and be a good mother. I expected this of myself without any of the skills or support I so desperately needed. To make things more confusing, at that time, in our culture, people did not value women staying at home. Women were going to work and creating careers for themselves. This served as a constant reminder of how my identity as a stay-at-home mom was not valued. My idea of being a mother still stemmed from the norms my mother's generation held. For me to enter the world of work and leave my children with someone I didn't know did not match with my idea of being a mom.

I thought if I could just try harder at doing what I thought was the right thing, everything would all work out. If I could just be a better wife and a good mother and sacrifice enough, everyone would finally recognize my value. It came as quite a blow to learn I wasn't making any progress because I wasn't taking responsibility for myself! Having the intentions to do the right thing was not enough. I often ignored what I needed to do because I did not listen to my own ability to access that voice inside of me that came from my faith in God. He equipped me with the ability to be a passionate, creative, capable woman, but I needed to claim what was already right inside of me.

When we were in Spokane, living in a small rental house, I came to know my worst fears were real. A woman called and asked for my husband. I had picked up on the extension in the bedroom and called out to him to pick up the phone out in the kitchen. As I stayed on the line, I could hear how startled and angry the woman's voice sounded when he answered. She wanted to know why he had not told her he was married and why he told her he loved her. He knew I was on the other line so he answered her with short, noncommittal responses that made her even angrier. She was sobbing as she hung up the phone. I was numb.

All along, I had had a sense of his disloyalty. He begged me to forgive him and said it would never happen again. That it was just a one-night stand. I knew better, but with two kids and a lot at stake, I decided to stick it out.

Before long, he was out most nights of the week and coming home at seven in the morning. It took me several months to find the courage to file for a divorce. I found a job and tried so hard to believe I could do it. But riddled with fear and guilt, I stopped the proceedings just before the papers became final. Later I learned that he lied to his parents, telling them he left me because I had an affair. My denial of who he was kept me stuck in the cycle for years to come.

By the time I delivered my third child, my physical health was beginning to break down. I came to find out later was it was the beginning of an immune disorder.

Because of my determination to keep taking care of everyone else, my own health had suffered. In trying to live this impossible life, I was making myself sick. I suffered from extreme fatigue, stomach problems, allergies, and sinus and hearing problems. I knew I needed to stop the behavior, but I didn't know how to begin. The false beliefs I held on to about taking care of others' needs over my own at all costs was not a healthy way to live. Not for me, my family, or anyone else.

My husband was a different person than who I had perceived he would be when I was sixteen years old. In my need to find love, I gave him attributes he did not possess. He did not see being a kind, faithful, caring partner the way I thought he would. He saw and lived in the world in a much different way. My distorted view of him did not match who he was or what he did. As long as I could take care of the children and go along with what he wanted, everything was fine. With each year, our backgrounds, our beliefs, our morals, and our values grew further apart. Even after he continued to drink, and as a result got a second assault charge when he put a man in the hospital for several days, a minister I went to for help told me to support my husband no matter what. I stayed.

My children and I were suffering but my martyrlike thinking kept me in denial and blinded me to the truth of what I was doing. I was under the misperception that

I could continue to cover up for his behavior with my kids by making excuses for him rarely being home or spending time with them. I thought I was doing them a favor. That could not have been further from the truth. Every time I covered up for him, I discounted and sabotaged myself.

Learning how to know I deserved more in my life would mean giving up everything that at one time I thought I needed to survive. It was like powerful magnets kept pulling me back to repeat old patterns. Yet something inside of me slowly began to shift. It began to surface through my vision of a better life and started to unfold as I set out to find a way to recover.

In time, I would come to know I couldn't figure it out on my own and I needed help…a lot of help! Upon the encouragement of my therapist, I started attending Co-Dependents Anonymous meetings. At first I felt so out of place. I was embarrassed and humiliated to attend and believed somehow I was different from all these "other people." Their problems were much worse than mine, and I didn't really belong in this place. I was sure this could not be happening to me. But it was. I could not hide behind the shame any longer, because the price I was paying was way too high.

There was a woman in my group who attended regularly but did not share any information about herself. When I had been with the group several months, she did begin to tell her own story, and the rest of us sat in amazement because of the pain in her history. When she finished that night, she said that she hadn't shared before because all of our issues were much worse. She felt her story was insignificant in comparison to ours!

This experience taught me not to compare stories but to hear and acknowledge each other, that it is through sharing and listening to one another that we can learn how to free ourselves. Somehow through opening ourselves we find hope and healing. It is an experiential process that over time builds us up and sets us free to learn how to live a full life. I find that this journey is lifelong, and I am still learning how to be open to the light that directs my path. For me, the group also grew to be a foster family, one where there was love, patience, kindness, acceptance, compassion, and all the things I needed to flourish as I grew.

In order to find the road to recovery, I would continue therapy and continue to attend the meetings for many years. I found lots of people there who lived through what I thought was only mine. I began to see how the years I spent isolating were harmful to me.

You Knew

He knew how to make promises he never kept
You knew how to love me
He knew how to work twelve hours a
day and make lots of money
You knew how to love me
He knew how to impress every-
one with his charisma and charm
You knew how to love me
He knew how to take my dreams
and turn them into stone
You knew how to love me

CHAPTER EIGHT: THE
DESIRE TO BE LOVED

For many years after I was married, sex was no longer a choice for me but an expectation. To say no was not an option. I was so young, and most of my experiences with men so far in my life had not been positive. As a result of the neglect I experienced as a child, along with watching and experiencing my father's abusive behavior and being exposed to his ongoing verbal abuse and intimidation, I lost something. It was like something inside didn't belong to me anymore, like I was different, altered. And with this, I found a conformity in how I was being treated. It was all I knew, what was familiar, a way of life—to be treated without regard for what I wanted or needed seemed normal. To express my needs and tell my husband no, to tell him to stop seemed impossible, because I would risk being hurt, abandoned, and alone. My father had never stopped when he beat my sister, so I could not imagine how I could make my husband stop. I believed this must be what I should accept. Since I had become pregnant, I felt that I did not deserve to express my needs. At this point there were no options, because this is what I brought upon myself. I needed to keep going and I did what I thought I had to do. I was having a baby and I needed to deal with it, suck up my own feelings, and go on, no matter what.

Our intimacy as a couple was connected to the shame I felt about myself and my family history. I know now that it is not uncommon for women who have suffered abuse or neglect as children to avoid revealing what is going on in their lives and their marital beds to anyone. Shame is handed down in a generational and visceral continuum that perpetuates a distorted interpretation of the truth.

It was also very hard for me when I was a little girl, and my sister would come home from the mental hospital and tell me about her experiences with men. Being exposed to the stories she would tell me was inappropriate and made a lasting impression on me in terms of how I came to see sexuality.

What happens in families often takes on a life of its own and lives itself out until someone changes the legacy. Somehow I convinced myself it was easier to live within the confines of the life I fell into than risk exposing what went on in our bedroom and face the shame. I was convinced it was my place to accept what was happening to me and that somehow that this was a way I needed to atone for the things I had done wrong. As mixed up as this may sound, it is the way I misperceived much of my environment.

Today I have a huge amount of empathy for that young woman who did not possess a concept of her own personhood. I am so grateful for the help available to women today through shelters, domestic hotlines, and support groups, where women can discover a sense of their inner power and their own creative spirit. I know that for me and so many other women, the isolation of those early years keeps us bound.

My own abuse will affect generations to come because I lived so many years blind to how it was permeating my life and how it stopped me from being able to distinguish my own needs, let alone the needs of my children. It is hard to recognize our behavior when our own filters for what is appropriate behavior are damaged and broken.

When I was so desperate to find the safety of a loving relationship, it was easy to give myself away, and once I did, it was next to impossible for me to step out of that position. Somehow the emotional suffering became so instinctive I could not recognize it. I just stepped out of me and into a persona who believed she had to just go on, detached from how she felt inside. I would not allow myself to share my true feelings, because I was so afraid that if anyone really knew me they would not want to be with me. My fear was that there must be something inherently wrong with me.

As our relationship continued to become more dysfunctional, I kept asking my husband to go to marriage counseling. Finally he agreed to attend a few times. Our sessions were difficult because of all we managed to ignore in the past. In previous sessions where I had gone by myself, I shared with the counselor that whenever I would tell my husband I did not want to have sex, it was not an option. So while we were in the middle of a session, the counselor looked directly at me and asked, "What is it like to be abused by your own husband?" He wanted me to face and deal with the implications of how what I was doing affected me. His question rocked me into reality and helped me face how I was hurting myself by not dealing with this part of my life. The question served as a wakeup call for me. My husband walked out of the session, but he did return for a few more sessions later to deal with some of his own history. I felt it was a breakthrough and hoped maybe we could begin to have an honest relationship.

The abuse had started early in our marriage when I was very young, pregnant, and feeling helpless. Going back home was not an option for me. My parents' marriage was still so fragile, and with my pregnant older sister living with them at the time, I thought I had nowhere to turn. There weren't a lot of options for pregnant teens in that era, and because of the shame that separated me from making better choices for myself, I felt trapped. I saw myself as abandoned, alone, and unlovable. The shame I continued to own reinforced the old voices in my head that told me I was not good enough and would never deserve more.

Initially shame is paralyzing and has a numbing effect on the victim. The more the victim is exposed to the abuse, the more it numbs the senses and separates him or her from the ability to make better decisions. I lived in this part of my life as if it were separate, excusing it as if what was happening were normal. When the counselor put the abuse into words, I could see the truth of what I was doing and what was happening to me. In time, I began to understand what all this would mean to me as a woman. Later in my life, I could begin to embrace the joy of being free and safe through a close, intimate relationship. As a woman, I would discover how to create and nurture a loving and faithful relationship with a partner. This brought an emotional and spiritual healing, with many changes to follow. The beauty of this would be the start of what was yet to come and signify a turning point in my life.

Because a very wise counselor chose to confront me with the question, I began to become more aware of my own body and reclaim myself. I started to feel more alive. In our relationship my own sexuality had been repressed because of the shame I carried, and I was unable to experience the joy of intimacy. The words the counselor said set me free to explore what was always mine: my own sexuality. There was a magic in speaking what until then was unspoken. That represented another part of how I would gradually learn to have my own voice and speak my own truth. It provided another pathway to continue on the road to recovery. I was amazed that, for the first time, I felt a sense of sexual freedom within me. It was like unlocking a door so I could walk through and know I did not have to fear what was on the other side. I could make choices about when and if I had sex and how I experienced my own gift to love and be loved.

Arise

She understands the call for she has heard it before
Now she knows its meaning
She hears it with new ears for she is ready to listen
She was deaf before
The words were lost in the pages of history
Now they are printed on the front page
and she runs to get her a copy
She is full of joy that bounces off the walls of her heart
She has begun her debut and the ap-
plause is rising in the air
You can't stop it for she is destined to claim what she lost
Eager to find out what is on the next page
The bold print that proclaims her freedom
The heights she is climbing
The health she is claiming
Now she can dance in the streets
and march in her parade
No need for the bands and the floats
Joy resides in her heart and pulses through her veins
Life has come
Sweet and precious

CHAPTER NINE: THE BEST AND THE WORST

Alaska is a place where survival is a big word. In Anchorage, the seasons are very different. It goes from winter to something Alaskans refer to as breakup and then what I would call spring and back to winter. One year, it was early September, the grass was still green, and the trees still had all of their leaves, and boom—we had two feet of snow. Breakup came around March or April, when the ice and snow started to melt. It was a welcome time of year, but it also revealed a mess when everything that had been frozen over winter thawed to reveal all the garbage underneath. Anything people had thrown out of car windows turned up. Sometimes very surprising things turned up, like people who had died of overexposure.

Just before we moved back to what Alaskans call the lower forty-eight, I went into the pharmacy to pick up a prescription. I knew the pharmacist well and when I told him we were moving he stated, "It is a good thing, because if you stayed any longer, you would have that Alaskan mentality." People who move to Alaska come to understand what that means. In the winter, it is dark most of the time and in the summer, mostly light. Living in the severe weather requires constant adaptations—both environmental and emotional.

I felt so separate from the continental US and so isolated from my family and friends. There is an odd feeling that comes from enduring life in a harsh climate and it is difficult to explain, but somehow I began to believe I could survive anything; it takes a certain mindset to tolerate the winters and stay. My beliefs about enduring my marriage were similar. It's one of those things you have to experience to fully understand, but once you have been there for a while—you do.

Just like the annual revelations of the season of breakup, dealing with the changes of living in Alaska for eight years revealed some things in our marriage that had been frozen for a long time. All the years in which I managed not to deal with my husband's choices about alcohol and multiple relationships with other women were catching up with me. Until this point, I had found ways to stay numb to what I was tolerating and was able to separate much of my life from his. It was as if a part of me lived on another continent. Since he was gone much of the time, I made a life of my own. I made excuses for him and just kept going.

Moving is a great way to avoid what is really going on in life. However, in 1981, our move to Anchorage would be the one that provided me with several opportunities to help me to grow and change. It was also where all the sacrifices of moving for my husband's career would culminate in him becoming the president of a company and reaching an income potential he had only dreamed would come. It would also end with a devastating incident for our oldest son, Chad.

So the move to Alaska came, as moves always did before, with a lot of sacrifices for the rest of us. It came when our oldest son was starting his junior year in a new high school—terrible timing—and our middle son had to begin another new school. Our youngest was starting kindergarten. We left everything: our home, friends, familiar places, and activities. These were precious treasures and parts of the foundation for us to have healthy lives as individuals and as a family. The emotional cost of this move rattled all of us and came with a price no amount of money could ever compensate.

I remember after moving there, I walked our youngest to his first day of school. When I turned to head home, the Chugach Mountains crossed the horizon. Laden with their first blanket of snow, they served as a stark reminder of where I was. It was like freefalling off the edge of the earth to come face to face with that moment. I knew I would need to sort out my future. I would need to figure out how to move into a new life again. I also knew that some things in my marriage kept getting neglected because of the many new life challenges that kept interrupting the inevitable. Moving served to keep me off balance and it also served to keep my husband's history from catching up with him. A history I refused to face and deal with that was full of lies and deceit.

At first I was a trooper, working hard to get the kids and myself oriented to another town, a different lifestyle, and a new culture and grounded again. I did my usual routine and found all the schools for the kids and got them registered and into sports. I took them to get ice skates and snow skis and signed them up for lessons to help us deal with the long winters. Together we learned how to navigate the city, started in a new church, and settled into another house and new neighborhood. During the next year, I signed up for a class at Anchorage Community College. My husband worked long hours, and we all made lives of our own.

The stress of the move was exhausting, but I was resolved to do the best I could. My immune disorder manifested itself in a diagnosis of ulcerative colitis and chronic sinus problems. After five days in the hospital to get the colitis under control and a sinus surgery a year later, I just kept going.

In time I attended a women's Bible study and started

meeting friends. While I was attending, a woman approached me and asked if I would like to serve in Christian Women's Club, a group I was familiar with and whose cause I appreciated. The club provided an opportunity for women to meet in a group and hear about how other women found their faith in God. Women came from all denominations and churches throughout the Anchorage area. When I inquired about what the position would be, she answered, "Chairperson for the group!" I was shocked and replied that I would have to rely completely on God to do this because I had never done anything like it before. She replied, "That is exactly what we are looking for!"

I knew she had observed me at the Bible study we both attended and it was obvious there was something about me that led her to believe I could do the position. But I was so surprised and all I could think to say was I would need two weeks to pray about it. When I returned to meet with her, I knew God would help me and I knew I wanted to give it a try.

For the next two years, I served as chairperson and found when I trusted God, He provided a bridge to hold me up. I loved being a part of something bigger than myself and watching what happened when I said yes to something I never thought I could do. The position offered me a variety of ways to learn about relationships and develop social skills. I know God could not have chosen anything more right for me.

As my faith grew, I began to change and started reading more and exploring my knowledge of God. Two books helped me: *Beyond Sex Roles: A Guide for the Study of Female Roles in the Bible,* by Gilbert Bilezikian, and *The Chalice and the Blade: Our History, Our Future,* by Riane Eisler. These two books gave me new insight about being a woman. They also helped expand my understanding of God and provided a means with which I could look at my beliefs from other perspectives. They provided something more too; they helped me to find freedom through my faith and be more tolerant of others' views and beliefs. These were huge steps toward gaining my own spiritual and emotional growth.

I started seeing a therapist who was also a minister and who possessed an ability to be kind yet direct. I was also attending the University of Alaska and had enrolled in a social work degree. The program served to increase my self-awareness and give me an understanding of myself. I began to understand and forgive myself for the choices I had made that were based on the beliefs I held onto as a child to survive. It helped me build the foundation for the developmental changes I needed to go through in order to change my life and make it better. It also helped me build the skills and tools I needed to have the career I longed for.

At the time, I was struggling with making a decision

to continue going to school. After a few sessions, the counselor looked me straight in the face and said, "Get your education," and I knew exactly what he meant! He was well aware my marriage was not going to make it and he believed in me and wanted me to be ready to end the relationship. He didn't have to say another word. Completing my master's degree and learning how to change my personal beliefs and evolve became decisions that would pave the way to my future.

Inspiration

Stars suspended in the universe
Hung there for you and for me
Inviting us to reach for them
So when we do
We will begin to reflect their glow
And reveal our gifts
So others can grow

CHAPTER TEN: A SUDDEN CHANGE IN PLANS

About this time, our oldest son Chad was in the military and assigned to the flight deck of the USS *Enterprise*, hooking catapults to jets. During duty he was involved in an accident that resulted in a severe head injury. He was airlifted to the hospital in San Diego where, in the next two and a half months, he would undergo several major brain surgeries.

I left Anchorage at 2:30 in the morning to be with Chad. I had no idea when I got on that plane that I would be living most of the next two and a half months in a forty-eight-bed head-injury ward in the San Diego Balboa Naval Hospital. I spent nights on a futon in my nephew Jim's apartment; he was living in San Diego while attending law school. I didn't know from one day to the next if Chad would survive. Early each day I would get in my little rental car from a company called Rent-A-Wreck, an appropriate name for what I felt I was going through.

Every day when I came back from spending all day at the hospital, I would be so angry about what was happening to Chad. I was so mad at God that this could happen. After all, didn't I always pray for my children's safety, do everything I could to serve God and be faithful? I wanted to tear something apart because I felt torn apart. Yet in the midst of all of this, I also knew God understood my rage. Each day, He revealed His love for me through the people who helped me. There is no way I would ever have been able to do this without my nephew Jim and his roommate's girlfriend, Alicia. One night after a tough day at the hospital, Alicia asked if she could massage my feet. She knew it had been a terrible day and I was exhausted. The gift of the massage was such a beautiful, clear example of how God was watching after me. I felt as if the angels came to me through the generous emotional support and gifts of precious time with Jim and Alicia. Their patience, love, and care for me provided an oasis in the midst of a horrible struggle.

Chad did survive, but life would never be the same. The results of his injury took several years of adjustment and treatment, and Chad suffered long-lasting complications. This incident placed me in the role of advocating for him and put everything else on hold. Just getting him released from the military was very difficult. Along the way, people told me to give it up. I could not. By the time he came home, I had contacted the governor, the state representative, the mayor, our senator, and our congressman to get him released. For some reason, Chad ended up on a light duty assignment at Naval Air Station Miramar. He would call us and express how depressed and confused he was about what was happening to him.

Ultimately, I was contacted by a representative in Washington DC, who made arrangements for me to take a flight to Miramar and have an appointment with Chad's commanding officer. Together we made the arrangements for Chad to come home. Soon after, he was released from the military. After extensive medical tests and treatment, Chad was granted full retirement from the military and full VA benefits.

The accident and the recovery period left another trail of adjustments for our whole family. When I left for San Diego in the middle of the night, I also left my two sons Jason and Nick with my husband in Alaska. Jason, whom I know took on most of the responsibilities at home, was in high school at the time, and Nick was only eight years old. I know this created a struggle for each of them. We all tried to regroup and heal, but there were deep emotional wounds for all of us. The accident left a trail of unresolved issues in our marriage that were once again put on hold. We struggled through our last year in Alaska.

Moving Again

IN 1989, THE COMPANY SENT US TO A SMALL TOWN NEAR the Canadian border. We lived in Bellingham, Washington, for about three years, and I attended Western Washington University while there. I was anxious to start college again to finish my degree. Whenever I changed schools, I typically lost credits. It was also unfortunate that this school did not have a degree in social work. So I ended up losing credits again when I changed to sociology as a major. The good news is that, after all those years, I received my BA in sociology from Western. Over the course of my degree and with all the moves, it was extremely difficult to get through the maze of credits. By the time I completed my master's degree, I had attended nine different colleges.

Throughout this time, there remained a powerful desire within me to find a way out of the life I had fallen into. It took relearning what I thought was "normal behavior" to gain the ability to put the pieces of my life back together in a new way. The most powerful resource I possessed was my faith in God, and interwoven through all the years, I was growing in my faith. The experiences I went through made me who I am today. I don't question that, and as difficult as it has been to go through them, there were also many adventures, rewards, and good memories to carry forward.

Change is hard, yet now I know it pushes me to become more. Now I can see how each move encouraged me to reach beyond myself and expand my ability to experience new things and relationships. Many of the struggles I went through became opportunities, and with each one I learned more about myself and life.

I had come from a small country town, where I thought I would stay the rest of my life. I found that God held a whole lot more in store for me and my family, that God was changing me and preparing me for more than I could have ever imagined. All along the way, I have been given the privilege of serving so many others through my profession, and I have met and been sustained by wonderful people, who supported me all along the way.

While we lived in Bellingham, I started to see another counselor and continued to go to Co-Dependents Anonymous meetings for support. When I first went to the meetings in this new location, I felt mortified and out of my comfort zone all over again. I didn't want anyone I knew to see me or think I needed help. After all, I was soon to graduate from college, a grown woman, and I should be beyond all this. The old shame from keeping everything secret and hiding what was going on in my life were powerful. But I kept going, because through therapy and the meetings I learned more about my skewed beliefs and how to develop and apply the new life skills I was learning. By this time, I knew the advantages of going far outweighed the disadvantages of not going. I knew I needed to trust taking the action to go instead of allowing my feelings of discomfort to keep me stuck. As people in the group shared their stories, I recognized their histories as being all too familiar. I realized I was not alone and learned from the group process to feel safe about exploring my history.

Learning to give myself loving compassion and treat myself with gentle kindness continues to help me gain the capacity to love others and myself. To learn the intricacies of listening to myself, slowing myself down, practicing how to be still, and paying attention to my own ability to feel led me forward. In this way I caught up with the person I desired and deserved to be. I also discovered who I waited to be for so long.

Love Abounds

Once meant to keep me safe
Old walls come down
Where there was no light
Now love abounds

CHAPTER ELEVEN:
THE LAST LIE

The last lie was different, because I was different. I was no longer willing to lie to myself in order to stay in a relationship. No longer willing to compromise who I was and who I wanted to be. All my life I held on to the belief that you must stay married no matter what. It was what my parents did, and I was determined to do the same.

THE DIVORCE

AFTER THIRTY-TWO YEARS, I COULD NOT FACE ANOTHER day of living in my marriage. I knew it was time to go through the divorce, despite what had held me back in the past. In my quest to make my marriage work, I had numbed myself to the truth. In doing that, I deceived myself. As long as I could deceive myself, I wouldn't have to leave. The truth was each time I numbed myself and put up with hurtful behaviors, I was betraying myself. When

I pushed ahead, believing I was doing the right thing and believing things would change, I was only putting off the inevitable. In tolerating and bearing the pain, I brought more pain and suffering for me and my family. I could not do it anymore. I could not go on deceiving myself.

At this point, I knew the opposite of what I believed all these years was true. It was not honest for me to stay in a marriage that was not working, and it was not working because I refused to recognize I was living a life where my own behavior abandoned not only myself but also my children. The honest thing to do would be to find my own life and discover what all this would mean. My fear of getting a divorce cost me so much more than the act of getting one. The pain of going through the divorce would be life-altering, and it needed to be. I needed to allow the pain in order to welcome a new life and a future. I filed for divorce.

After thirty-two years of marriage, my husband and I got up and started to get ready for work. We had talked the night before about ending the marriage, and just before he left for work, he came over to ask me if I was mad at him. I was thinking, "What in the hell are you asking such a ridiculous question like that for?" We kissed goodbye and he left for what would be the last day we would live together.

A New Legacy

WHAT FOLLOWED WOULD CHANGE THE LEGACY OF MY

life. Ending my marriage was the hardest thing I ever did and the most honest thing I would ever do. With time I came to experience my life to hold a quality unknown to me before. Because of the decision to end my marriage, I moved forward into a life that continues to reward and validate that decision.

Holding onto the beliefs I used to survive when I was young, despite how they affected my life, did not serve me well into my adulthood. During the years I swallowed the pain and sorrow of what was happening to me, I also swallowed my own voice. When I claimed my voice, I moved forward into the life God prepared me to live. I shed my childish beliefs and discovered a power waiting within me that led me forward into an incredible life. One where I established a career to move into the profession I had only dreamed of before. As an adult woman, I embraced what had always been within me and discovered I had everything I needed. Through my personal development and faith, I recognized the gifts within me and claimed them.

Lies are destructive and they are insidious. They creep in and devour what is precious and good. I decided to stop the lies. Stop telling them to myself and stop believing the lies my partner was telling me. The blessings of this decision stand before me each day. They are a testament to my choice as I experience the emotional freedom to love and be loved.

My ability to grow into adulthood is a lifelong challenge. It requires me to acknowledge the consequences of the decisions I make so I can be honest with myself and with others. In my quest to not feel emotional pain and push it away, I am, in essence, choosing to live in fear. I am blind to my own abilities to cope. When I allow myself to experience feelings, I find they can pass through and I can step into my own expression of what God wants for me. I know He wants joy for me. I claim that today.

Staying numb for so many years kept me from creating a better life. It held me captive and separated me from experiencing the abundant life I know now. As long as I continued to live out the old legacy, I could neither see the options before me nor experience the gifts I possessed to invest in my personal growth. While living in fear, I stayed paralyzed in my life and unable to embrace my own value and a sense of the creative spirit, beauty, and talent within me.

Life is full of wonder when we possess the emotional freedom to live it no longer clinging to someone else for authenticity and instead claiming the power of what frees us from within: an eternal creative spirit. For when we come to find ourselves, we are capable of uniting with the community of others who are striving to know and experience their purpose as well. It is then that we can become a living force together as we are present to the goodness and light of God in our lives.

In My Dreams

Somehow in my dreams you came
And filled an empty space with love
Gave me a reason to breathe
For the sun to shine, the moon to glow

CHAPTER TWELVE: LUCKY ME

The way I faced the last lie was by coming to recognize I had everything I needed. Through the years after the divorce, I built my future. I quit a job that was not the right fit for me and went from part-time to full-time in my own private practice. Within a short period of time, my business tripled in size and I became financially independent. I built my own home and created a new life. Just for fun, I started going out with friends and taking dance lessons. I enjoyed my grandchildren and got acquainted with neighbors. I went on some trips with other single people from my church.

I also started to join group activities for singles and participated in some hikes, golf, dance, and other social gatherings. It was awkward to be around other men and uncomfortable. But I wanted to make some friends outside of the ones from my marriage and knew I would need to push myself to get out of my comfort zone.

And then something unexpected happened. At three p.m. one day, I walked into the lobby of the Heathman

Hotel and spotted him sitting on the leather sofa facing the fireplace. Months before, my dear friend Bonnie and I were talking over dinner with my cousin Susan and Susan's husband. Susan's husband had challenged us to start dating and recommended the personal ads, which in the late nineties were still popular as a dating resource. We both laughed at him, but he convinced us, saying he and my cousin would help us figure out how to write them and it would be fun. By the end of the evening, after much laughter and banter, our ads were done. My girlfriend and I challenged each other to place the ads. Whoever did it first, the other had to follow suit. When she left, I stuffed mine into the drawer and forgot about it, thinking neither of us would ever pursue such a ridiculous idea. But a couple of months later, I decided to take on the challenge.

The afternoon I walked into the Heathman, I felt ready to take a risk and meet someone. The previous two meetings with other men had been complete bombs, lasting about ten minutes each. I was pretty discouraged. So when I spotted him in the crowded lobby, the only person sitting alone and looking around as if he were searching for someone, I paused. I thought to myself, "What in the hell am I doing? I am about to meet a man I know nothing about and I could easily turn around and walk out." Just as quickly as the thought came, another replaced it and I heard myself asking, "What do I have to lose?" I walked over and introduced myself, and we went to get a table.

What I thought would be a few minutes turned into a few hours. His calm manner and the warm tone of his voice comforted something inside me and flowed over me like cool water folds over smooth rock. With him there was no pretense, and it was clear to me he wasn't a player looking for a one-night stand. We just shared kind words and conversation; we were two people looking for a connection. An hour later, we left the hotel to go for a walk along the Columbia River. We wanted get to know more about each other, and at the same time, we were talking as if we already did. We freely shared our values with regards to family, faith, education, and interests. It didn't take long to recognize that we wanted to see each other again.

Over the next few weeks, we golfed, went out for meals together, took long walks, and met one another's families. Our first trip to the beach, we both knew what we wanted. After just a few months, we were together and life took on a quality of intimacy never known to us before. There was no question about how lucky we both felt. We loved each other from the start and reveled in the experience. We continue to know that joy after twelve years of marriage.

Life with my husband Lyle is like the flip side of the relationship in my first marriage. My first husband was always on the make or on the take. I lived my life with him yearning for any emotional connection and sense of trust.

Life with Lyle is like a knowing. There is a big difference when you are with someone whom you never doubt loves you. When you know if you fall, fail, or screw up what you will get back is encouragement, compassion, and kindness. The quality and comfort this brings to my life is the polar opposite of what I knew before and brings me peace instead of chaos. He is a constant. I know I am loved and cared for and I can count on him. When conflict comes, we endeavor to regulate our own emotions and find options to resolve issues. We fight fair and don't resort to putting each other down, refusing to talk, yelling, or name-calling. Neither of us look for a quick fix, like resorting to using coping strategies that would harm our relationship. It is like living in a different world. Our energy together is devoted and clear.

This brings a quality to life I never experienced before and provides a calm place to land. We endeavor to sustain one another, lift each other up, and consider the needs of our partner as equal to our own. We bring our personal gifts to the relationship and continue to help one another grow and evolve. We have a deep appreciation for slowing down and being present in our lives and we take time to pay attention to one another's need for support and affirmation. Having a partner who possesses the ability to be close on an emotional level creates a place of encouragement to grow in my own interests, goals, and dreams. He encourages me to take time to be with friends or complete projects that are important to me. We take time to pray together every day and support each other in our need to grow spiritually and find ways to increase our understanding of God in our lives. It took me a long time to learn to trust again and it took a patient and empathetic partner to help me learn how.

Six years ago, we found some land in the Columbia Gorge and built a small cottage. It sits on a hill with a beautiful view of Mount Adams to the northwest, and behind us rise the Columbia Hills. We are surrounded by oak, pine, and fir trees that cover the thirteen acres and offer us a secluded place to get away. The cottage has provided a place for me to get the time to write this book, be inspired by nature, and recover from the stress of the world. Lyle has time there to create a garden of beautiful ornamental grasses, bamboo, and the over two hundred trees he planted. Beautiful pines, firs, and sumac that started out less than a foot tall now average around five feet in height. The cottage also provides a place for us to be together in a secluded setting where we can slow down, shift gears, and enjoy our love for one another and for the earth God has given us. We feel like love came to find us, wrapped its arms around us, and gave us a second chance.

I recognize now the traumas in my life needed time to heal, and I needed to do things to help myself reconnect because I had left parts of me behind. The trauma I experienced left me disconnected in so many ways. Through the love of dear friends and my husband I have built my awareness and taken action to intentionally seek the help

I needed.

The divorce helped me get my life back. Some of the things I did to help me heal are the same things I encourage others to do. Make new friends, seek out professional help, be willing to try different experiences, take risks in creating a successful future, learn from the experts how to change your life with a variety of resources, replace old beliefs and negative self-talk by developing a new positive voice, and become aware of how to be present in your life.

I know I have a lot more to learn and I also know I am capable of doing so. That makes all the difference. I make a decision every day to continue to grow myself into wholeness. I will always be grateful to my dear friends and family. I am especially thankful for my husband, Lyle, who over the years spent hours with me as I worked to regain health. I will be eternally grateful for their loving kindness and for how they went beyond what was imaginable. They helped me heal through their patience, kindness, empathy, perseverance, and love. They each taught me what love is. They have served as the models of loving kindness I needed to move forward and leave the past behind. Today I am so lucky to have the ability to encourage others to grow and do the same.

Learning to Breathe

As I stop to take a breath
I collide with time
And surrender to my own awareness
Where the moment can intertwine

EPILOGUE: OLD DRAGONS

Recently I watched the movie *Alice in Wonderland* with Johnny Depp. In one scene, Alice is running up a seemingly endless spiral of stairs with a huge saber in her hand. She is in hot pursuit of a very ugly, very scary, enormous dragon. With each step, I can see the stairs are crumbling away from under her feet. For a split second, she looks back to notice the staircase is collapsing and disappearing behind her, but she is swift to turn and look ahead, despite her fear of falling into mid-air. She commits herself to going forward. The more she keeps her eyes on the goal, the more she is determined to accomplish her dream. In the end, she not only kills the dragon, she chops off its head!

My dragon comes to visit now and then when I least expect it, and it catches me off guard. It surprises me with something that triggers old emotional pain still floating around in the visceral part of my body. The dragon seems to come when I feel a sense of rejection or fear and find myself sad and doubtful. Just when I think I have that darn dragon under wraps, I'm facing it again. It particularly likes to attack when I am sad and feel overwhelmed. Like when I have a strong urge to control and fix a situation right away so I can stop my discomfort. It can take me a while to recognize and face that dragon again, so I remind myself to take a few moments to feel what is going on inside of me instead of pushing my feelings away. When I acknowledge and feel what is going on inside, instead of feeling like I am face to face with the dragon again, I can just listen to the feelings, allow myself to sense them, quiet my body, talk myself through them, and let go. That way the dragon does not have the power to fill me so full of fear I can't think for myself.

So even as my old ways of thinking are falling away from me like those steps fell away from under Alice's feet, I commit to moving forward. I know this is how I can come to deal with the dragon for what it is. This does not come easy for me. I tend to want to stay in my comfort zone, where I can neglect or refuse to deal with the dragon. It just feels much more "normal" to me. My old belief is if I can keep things the same and try to avoid any emotional discomfort, I will be safe. This makes it so difficult to take a look at what I am avoiding and only leads to more insecurity, lack of self-confidence, anger, guilt, resentment, or a variety of other issues to keep me locked into a life I do not want.

As a child I invented an emotional escape hatch. It

was a place to disappear to internally. As long as I was there, I thought I was invisible and no one could hurt me. It was easy to disappear in my family, since everyone was so preoccupied and no one seemed to notice, but this only served to reinforce the behavior that in the future did not serve me well as a positive coping strategy. To disappear internally I needed to shut myself off on an emotional level, disconnect from myself. When I did that, I lost myself, gave up my own identity, and gave up on my basic needs. When I kept using the behavior, I became a master at creating the illusion that everything was just fine. I repeated this because I thought it would help me survive—and for many years it did. I found this habit came close to killing me. I neglected my own body to the point of abandonment.

In my practice I can identify this behavior with clients when their eyes glaze over and they become vacant, unable to be present. They do this to leave moments or events that might cause them to feel the negative emotions they associate with earlier traumas.

For many years I believed, "I got this far by myself and I don't need anyone." This belief rendered me helpless in confronting and dealing with my own dragons. But as I start to recognize and acknowledge my own emotional needs, I gain inner strength to sort out the challenges and equip myself to see and understand new more productive ways to cope and trust. For unless I challenge and explore my feelings and beliefs, I miss out on gaining the wisdom to move forward in my own evolution on this planet.

I am learning that when I am trapped in my own fear, I can't see the dragon for what it is. In my desperation to hold onto my beliefs, I settle for less and continue to live hanging precariously onto the edge of my goals. When I learn to face my fear, I gain momentum and move on to claim my vision. Each time I put this to the test, I am rewarded. And each time I move forward in faith, I am so blessed.

Putting my self-care first takes commitment and discipline. It does not just come naturally for me and takes practice. It took a long time for me to understand that as an adult, it would take giving myself permission to love myself to be able to attain the capacity to love others. The commitment to take care of myself pays off in dividends. For as I practice giving myself loving compassion, I can learn how to love others. As I teach myself to nurture me, I become more capable of giving this same love.

As a child, I did not learn how to take care of my emotions. As an adult, I can learn how through practice. Doing this is a personal investment that allows me to be open to new life experiences. So instead of demanding perfection of myself and others, I strive to listen, hear, and understand. Instead of numbing myself when conflict comes, I strive to stay present for myself and others. Instead of running away from conflict, I make a conscious choice about my behavior in order to regulate myself internally and keep my emotions in check. This helps me be more open to others and how I respond to them.

To gain a better life, I learned how to invest in fine-tuning my awareness of how to be present in each day. Through this investment, I begin to open and discover the value of what that discipline brings me. The practice of being present can still seem uncomfortable, strange, and awkward, but I am learning to accept the fact that it is okay to feel these feelings and they will pass. Again and again I find myself inviting my mind to be still so I can take a moment to travel within and tap into the resources I possess. This practice runs contrary to what the world seems to want me to do. The world wants me to believe I need to be in constant motion, pursuing quick ways to fix my emotions. But I know the returns of getting to trust and pay attention to what I have learned brings a peace and joy that nothing else can.

Learning new ways to become mindful of my own needs allows me to make better decisions about how I invest in my future. People who knew me in the past are often surprised at decisions I make now. Their kind validation and encouragement helps me to know I am headed in the right direction.